JANUA LINGUARUM

STUDIA MEMORIAE
NICOLAI VAN WIJK DEDICATA

edenda curat
C. H. VAN SCHOONEVELD
Indiana University

Series Minor, 198

INVARIANT ORDERING

by

GERALD A. SANDERS

University of Minnesota

1975
MOUTON
THE HAGUE · PARIS

ISBN: 90 279 3353 7

Printed in The Netherlands by Mouton & Co., The Hague.

PREFACE

This study presents evidence of the empirical viability and explanatory value of the Invariant Order Constraint as a universal principle of natural-language grammar. This constraint constitutes the central hypothesis of the general theory of Derivational Ordering, first outlined in my paper "Constraints on Constituent Ordering" (*Papers in Linguistics* 2 [1970], 460-502). Chapter 1 of the present study closely follows the introductory section of that paper. Chapters 2, 3, and 4 are, except for minor revisions, essentially identical to the papers entitled "Invariant Ordering" which appeared in duplicated form in February 1969 (Department of Linguistics, University of Texas at Austin) and March 1970 (Bloomington: Indiana University Linguistics Club). Selected portions have also been presented in public lectures at Indiana University in September 1967, and at the Summer Meeting of the Linguistic Society of America, Columbus, Ohio, July 25, 1969.

Research for this study was supported in part by a grant for the academic year 1968-1969 under the NSF Science Development Program in Language and Behavior, the University of Texas at Austin. I am grateful to Andreas Koutsoudas for valuable comments on the preliminary manuscript, and have also benefitted from the discussion of various ordering problems with Emmon Bach, Zev Bar-Lev (R. W. Lefkowitz), Mushira Eid, Linda Norman, Gunter Schaarschmidt, and James H.-Y. Tai.

Minneapolis
March 1973

TABLE OF CONTENTS

INTRODUCTION

Grammars of natural languages specify symbolic equivalence relations between the empirically-interpretable semantic and phonetic representations of linguistic objects. For all theories of grammar, it is assumed as an empirical condition for adequacy that the terminal phonetic representation of every linguistic object must include, for at least some of its constituents, an explicit specification of their relative linear ordering. Each such specification is interpreted into an observation statement of the form "X is initiated prior to Y", where X and Y are the articulatory states or events constituting the interpretations of phonetic constituents.

For terminal semantic representations, on the other hand, no such empirical condition is imposed, since there is no evidence of significant temporal precedence relations between the psychological states or events constituting the interpretation of semantic constituents. Nor does there appear to be any other observable semantic relation which might serve as a possible non-articulatory interpretation of the linear ordering relation in linguistic representations. The task then for all theories of grammar is to provide a principled basis for the correct specification of ordering relations in phonetic representations and for the correct pairings of such significantly ordered representations with semantic representations, which are not significantly ordered, either in the same sense or in any other known sense.

Alternative approaches to this task are determined by alternative assumptions concerning the derivational predictability, variability, and terminal completeness of the ordering relations that hold

between linguistic constituents. Evidence presented here and elsewhere (e.g. Sanders 1967, 1972) provides empirical support for the claim that the most general and most revealing grammatical theories are those which assume that all terminal phonetic elements are ordered and that all linguistic ordering relations are derivationally predictable and invariant under transformation or substitution of linguistic representations. These restrictions follow from the following three universal constraints on grammatical derivations:

(1) the SEMANTIC COMPLETENESS CONSTRAINT — that all constituents of terminal semantic representations are related to each other by GROUPING (a symmetric relation) and NOT by ORDERING (an antisymmetric relation);

(2) the PHONETIC COMPLETENESS CONSTRAINT — that all constituents of terminal phonetic representations are related to each other by ORDERING and NOT by GROUPING;

(3) the INVARIANT ORDER CONSTRAINT — that if an element token A precedes an element token B in any line of a given derivation, then there is no line in that derivation in which B precedes A.

These general constraints, which contribute significantly to the natural delimitation of natural language and natural-language grammar, actually follow in turn from metatheoretical principles of a still more general and essentially definitional character. Thus the two Completeness Constraints can in fact be derived simply from the general formal definition of an interpretable representation as a string of property and relational elements which are each uniquely interpretable in the same extratheoretical mode or domain. For linguistic theories, this means that nothing can count as a terminal, or interpretable, representation of a linguistic object unless its elements are either all uniquely interpretable into non-null observation statements about cognition or else all uniquely interpretable into non-null observation statements about articulation. Since there appears to be no unique non-null articulatory interpretation for grouping and no unique non-null cognitive interpretation for ordering, it follows that there can be no grouping specifications in terminal phonetic representations and no ordering specifications in terminal semantic representations.

The Invariant Order Constraint can likewise be viewed simply as a necessary implication of the defining antisymmetric, or non-commutativity, axiom for ordering relations. Thus to say that the constituents of any representation [X & A & B & Y] are ordered means that for any non-identical A and B [X & A & B & Y] and [X & B & A & Y] are non-equivalent. Since the lines of any grammatical derivation, or proof of a given sound-meaning pairing, constitute an equivalence class of linguistic representations (see Sanders 1972), it follows then that [X & A & B & Y] and [X & B & A & Y] cannot be representations of the same linguistic object, and hence cannot possibly cooccur as lines of the same derivation.

Our actual concern here, however, is not with the logical basis and metatheoretical naturalness of these general constraints on constituent ordering, but rather with their strictly empirical implications and their specific values in motivating and directing the expression of significant explanatory generalizations about natural languages. The focus for the present study will be the Invariant Order Constraint. Its empirical appropriateness will be argued in the following chapters by showing with respect to several critical test cases that the limitations on grammars imposed by the principle of Invariant Ordering are consistent with highly valued explanations of the facts in question. The remainder of the present chapter will be devoted to the establishment of a metatheoretical foundation for the comparison of theories that observe and do not observe the general constraints of the derivational ordering hypothesis.

In order to make any real comparison of alternative theories, there must be some single theory or metalanguage to which each of the alternatives can be accurately reduced. The joint reduction of all alternative theories of ordering can be adequately achieved by means of a theory which assumes that there are two and only two distinct relations which may hold between the constituents of linguistic representations, and one and only one schema for rules mapping instances of one relation into instances of the other.

The two relations that will be assumed are ones that nearly all grammarians have taken to be jointly necessary for the adequate

description of natural languages. These relations are distinctively different both in their formal properties as relations and in their empirical interpretations.

The first relation is symmetric, or commutative, and has the rough interpretation 'is (cognitively or psychologically) associated with'. We will call this relation GROUPING, or co-constituency, and will symbolize it by a comma between bracketed arguments. Thus, for any constituents A and B, [A, B] = [B, A].

The second relation that may hold between linguistic constituents is antisymmetric, or non-commutative, and has the empirical interpretation 'precedes', or 'is initiated prior to'. This relation, usually known as ORDERING, or linear concatenation, will be symbolized here by an ampersand between arguments. Thus, for any (non-identical) constituents A and B, [A & B] ≠ [B & A].

Given the relations of grouping and ordering, we can now formally define an ORDERING RULE as any statement of the form

$$X [A, B] Y = X [A \& B] Y$$

where X and/or Y may be null and where A and B are both constituents, i.e. bracketed strings that are free of unpaired brackets.

Each ordering rule expresses an empirical generalization about the order of the constituents of some grammatical construction. Thus, for example, the rule [[DET], [NOUN]] = [[DET] & [NOUN]] expresses the generalization that in constructions consisting of a determiner and a noun it is always the case that the determiner precedes the noun. (This rule holds for Chinese, English, French, etc., but not, of course, for languages like Malay or Thai, in which determiners follow rather than precede their nouns.) Each such rule determines a pair of converse intermodal, or lexical, substitution transformations which justify derivational mapping relations between pairs of linguistic representations, or phrase-markers, that differ only in the nature of the relational element which is associated with a certain specified pair of constituents. Like other rules of grammar, therefore, each ordering rule is empirically justifiable in terms of its specific contributions to the general mapping function that specifies the proper pairings

between the interpretable semantic representations of linguistic objects and their interpretable phonetic representations.

This general metatheory, with its two relations and one inter-relational mapping schema, is sufficient for the reduction of all possible theories of constituent ordering. It is thus possible in this framework to deal with the alternative assumptions of these theories in an entirely explicit and notationally uniform manner.

Concerning the PREDICTABILITY of ordering relations, there are only three logically-possible alternatives: either no orderings are predictable, or else all orderings are predictable, or else some but not all are predictable. Ordering would be WHOLLY UNPREDICTABLE in some language if and only if, for any [A & B] in its phonetic representations, [A & B] is not in the range of any possible true ordering rule. (It goes without saying that there is no natural language which has this property, and even an artificial language of this sort is difficult to conceive. Thus, for example, even for a language with complete random ordering and random bracketing of terminal constituents, every ordered pair of constituents will still fall within the range of a true ordering rule, namely, the maximally general rule $[X, Y] = [X \& Y]$, where X and Y are unrestricted variables for any constituents.) Ordering would be PARTLY PREDICTABLE in some language if and only if there is at least one [A & B] in its phonetic representations which is in the range of a true ordering rule, and at least one [C & D] which is not in the range of any such rule. Ordering would be COMPLETELY PREDICTABLE, finally, if and only if EVERY [A & B] is in the range of some true ordering rule.

For constituents down to the size of morphemes at least, there appears to be no evidence which might lead one to doubt the claim that ordering is completely predictable in all languages. Complete predictability of the ordering of syntactic constituents has in fact been explicitly recognized already in the traditional literature, both for superficial representations (Hockett 1954) and for those at the intermediate level of syntactic deep structure (Chomsky 1965). For most phonological constituents too, ordering appears to be generally predictable from given specifications of constituents

and their groupings. But even where general prediction of this sort appears to be impossible — as, for example, for the syllables of certain idioms and polysyllabic names like *snapdragon* or *Mississippi* — correct prediction can still be effected by the lexical rules for such structures, whose phonological members would simply include specifications of all those ordering relations that cannot be derived by more general rules referring to phonological constituents and constituency relations alone. It is not the mere POSSIBILITY of prediction which is of interest, however, since it is possible to predict almost anything, given enough assumptions and initial conditions. Rather, what makes the predictability of ordering relations significant is the independence and naturalness of the required initial conditions — constituents and their associations — and the conceptual and explanatory generality of the predictive principles themselves — the general ordering rules that are required for the specification of correct orderings for all constructions.

Given the standard empirical conditions that at least some terminal phonetic elements are ordered and that at least some terminal semantic elements are grouped, there are only four possible assumptions about the COMPLETENESS of the relations holding between constituents of terminal linguistic representations. Thus phonetic representations must be either completely or partially ordered, and semantic representations must be either completely or partially grouped. (Since all element pairs are assumed to be either grouped or ordered, partial grouping implies partial ordering, and vice versa.) For theories that observe neither of the completeness constraints, semantic and phonetic representations are relationally non-distinct, both being strings of elements that are partially ordered and partially grouped. For theories that observe both of these constraints, these two modes of terminal representation are mutually exclusive not only in their constituent property or categorial elements but also in the relations that hold between them.

There appears to be no presently known clear evidence against either of the two completeness constraints. Moreover, the only

possible way of falsifying them would appear to be by demonstrating that some states in the proper cognitive renditions of sentences are SIGNIFICANTLY ORDERED, or that some states in their proper articulatory renditions are SIGNIFICANTLY SIMULTANEOUS. Pending such evidence, therefore, it is reasonable to consider both of the completeness principles to be true, since they determine a smaller class of possible grammars than their contradictories, and have a much greater capacity to motivate and direct the search for significant generalizations about languages.

Concerning the derivational VARIABILITY of ordering relations, finally, there are only two possible assumptions: Ordering is either invariant in derivations, or else it is variable. The latter assumption allows for the possibility of rules effecting the derivational reordering, or permutation, of constituents; the former precludes any such rules. Theories that incorporate the Invariant Order Constraint thus determine a more restricted class of possible grammars and grammatical derivations than can be determined by any otherwise equivalent theories that are inconsistent with this constraint.

However, though clearly distinctive with respect to strong generative capacity, the contradictory assumptions of variable and invariant ordering do not appear to differ with respect to weak generative capacity, at least for the sets of ordered terminal phonetic representations that they are consistent with. Thus, for example, the effect of any ordering and subsequent reordering of constituents, as determined by the rules of (G.1), will always be identical to the effects of a pair of simple ordering rules, like those of (G.2).

(G.1)   (i)   [A, B] = [A & B]
        (ii)   X [A & B] Y = X [B & A] Y
(G.2)   (i)   X [A, B] Y = X [B & A] Y
        (ii)   [A, B] = [A & B]

(The required applicational precedence of (i) over (ii) of (G.2) follows from the forms of the rules by the universal principle of Proper Inclusion Precedence [Sanders 1970].) Similarly, the effects of any invariant ordering of [A, B] as [A & B] by a single ordering

rule will always be achievable in a manner that violates the Invariant Order Constraint — i.e. by a set of rules justifying the ordering of [A, B] as [B & A] and the reordering of [B & A] to [A & B], either by simple permutation or by sequential identity adjunction and deletion.

It is evident, therefore, that, unlike the two completeness constraints, the principle of Invariant Ordering cannot be confirmed or disconfirmed on the basis of any direct observation of the sounds or meanings of linguistic objects. The choice between the contradictory assumptions of variable and invariant ordering can in fact be made only on the basis of the explanatory range and generality of the grammars and grammatical theories that they are respectively consistent with. On this basis existing evidence appears to consistently favor the assumption of invariance. A selected sample of such evidence will be presented in the remaining chapters of this study.

This evidence will be presented through consideration of three critical tests of the empirical adequacy and explanatory value of the Invariant Order Constraint. All three tests involve relatively familiar data that have been explicitly dealt with in the recent literature by means of theories with the power of derivational reordering. The first test (Chapter 2) involves a set of facts about verbally reduced coordinations first dealt with by J. R. Ross (1970) in his paper "Gapping and the Order of Constituents". The second (Chapter 3) concerns the body of data affected by Ross's (1967) Complex NP Constraint. The third test (Chapter 4) involves the facts about coreferential nominal alternations dealt with by P. M. Postal's (1971) proposed Crossover Constraint. For all three of these cases, it will be shown that there are alternative explanations of the facts in question that are fully consistent with the Invariant Order Constraint and of greater generality and explanatory value than the variable order accounts that were originally proposed.

TEST I: VERBALLY REDUCED COORDINATIONS

The hypothesis of invariant ordering would be falsified if it could be shown that there are some linguistic facts which can be adequately accounted for only if it is assumed that there are two or more distinct orderings of the same constituents in the derivation of some single linguistic object. There would appear to be only two possible types of argument that might be used to demonstrate the necessity for such derivational variability in ordering. The first type of argument would involve a demonstration that the sequential application of rules to alternate orders of the same constituents is necessary for the principled explanation of some significant fact about some language. The second, and inherently much stronger, type of argument would involve a demonstration of the explanatory necessity of some general constraint on the reordering of some but not all grammatical constituents, the applicability and filtering function of such a constraint being dependent of course on the existence of rules which do in fact effect the reordering of some constituents.

The strongest rule-sequence argument for reordering that I know of is that presented by J. R. Ross in a recent paper entitled "Gapping and the Order of Constituents" (Ross 1970). Various movement-constraints have also been proposed by Ross (1967) and others, with perhaps the strongest argument for a constraint of this type having been provided by P. M. Postal in his recent study of coreferential "crossover" phenomena (Postal 1971). In the case of Ross's rule-sequence evidence for reordering, I will attempt to show here that reordering rules are of no explanatory value what-

ever and that the facts which he deals with can be accounted for in a more general and revealing way by assuming axiomatically-unordered underlying structures and invariant ordering rules. In the case of the apparent movement-constraint evidence presented by Ross and Postal I will merely present certain reasons for concluding that Ross's "Complex NP" constraint, and Postal's "crossover" constraint, like other purported movement-constraints, can be most appropriately formulated as constraints, not on the ordering or reordering of constituents, but rather on their associativity, or derivational re-grouping.

Ross's study (1970) is concerned with the explanation of certain facts about the possible forms of reduced coordinations in natural languages resulting through the process of identical verb deletion. This process, which Ross calls "gapping", is a special case of the general process of coordinative reduction, a process which has been discussed in various of its aspects in such recent studies as those of Gleitman (1965), Lakoff and Peters (1966), Postal (1968), Sanders (1967), Schane (1966), and Tai (1969). However, since both Ross's principal generalizations about verb deletion and the explanation of these generalizations that I am proposing here can be extended in a very straightforward way to other types of reduced coordinations, we can restrict our attention to the particular set of facts cited by Ross without diminishing the general significance of the explanatory issues involved.[1]

---

[1] Several important problems associated with coordination reduction will not be dealt with at all here. These include (1) the specification of the superficial grouping or regrouping of constituents in the products of coordination reduction; (2) the lexicalization and ordering of the conjunctive (AND) and disjunctive (OR) markers in reduced and unreduced coordinations; and (3) the derivation of discontinuous phrasal coordinations with *respectively* and their relations to ordinary continuous reductions. The problem of grouping has been discussed in some of its aspects by Koutsoudas (1971), Postal (1968), Ross (1970), Sanders (1972), Schane (1966), Tai (1969), and others; here it will be assumed that reductions affect the IDENTIFICATION of constituents but not their BRACKETING (see Ch. 4), and that any empirically-motivated adjustments in the grouping of the constituents of reduced coordinations will be effected by general bracket-elimination conventions of the sort discussed in Chapter 4. Since both conjunctive and disjunctive markers can be predicted from axiomatically unconnected coordinations that are represented in an alphabet that includes a negativity

Ross reports two fundamental observations about verbally-reduced coordinations in natural languages. First, while various languages exhibit one or more of the following superficial patterns of reduction,

(1) (a) SVO and SO
     (b) SOV and SO
     (c) SO and SOV,

it is apparently the case that no language has reductions of the form

(2) *SO and SVO.

(The symbols S, V, and O signify superficial subject, verb, and verbal complement or object, respectively.[2]) The three occurring patterns are exemplified by sentence (3 a, b, c), respectively:

(3) (a) I drank water, and Anna vodka   (SVO and SO)
     (b) Ja vodu pil, i Anna vodku   (SOV and SO)
          Russian: 'I water drank, and Anna vodka'
     (c) Ja vodu, i Anna vodku pila   (SO and SOV)
          Russian: 'I water, and Anna vodka drank'

Ross's second observation concerns the co-occurrence of these reduction patterns in particular languages. On this basis, four language-types are found:

---

element (see Sanders 1967: Secs. 4.3, 4.4), and since the ordering and lexicalization of these derived connective constituents can be specified in an entirely regular way upon the products of all coordination reduction processes, no reference need be made here to the connective properties of any sentences undergoing reduction. (For expository purposes, however, the word *and* will sometimes be included in the representations of ordered structures to mark the sentential boundary at which an overt connective may appear.) For discussion of *respectively*-constructions, see especially McCawley (1968), Postal (1968), and Tai (1969).

There are a number of incorrect factual claims made in Ross (1970) that will also be ignored here, since they are not directly relevant to the issues of present concern. For identification and correction of some of these claims, see Koutsoudas (1971), Pulte (1971), and Sanders and Tai (1972).

[2] These symbols are to be understood as expository abbreviations for the distinctive properties and/or grouping characteristics of these types of constituents. More formal characterizations will be provided in Chapter 4.

(4)	*English-type*:	SVO and SO
	Japanese-type:	SO and SOV
	Russian-type:	SVO and SO
		SOV and SO
		SO and SOV
	Hindi-type:	SOV and SO
		SO and SOV

The problem then is to account for these four sets of reductions and for the non-occurrence in any of them of the logically-possible reduction (2) *SO and SVO. For English- and Japanese-type languages, it is readily apparent that there is a direct relationship between the superficial order of constituents in the unreduced clauses of a language and that in its reduced coordinations. Actually, or course, there are several distinct but co-variant relations that hold here, and it is our task to determine which of these is primary and which are secondary, which relation expresses a significant linguistic generalization and which are merely necessary consequences of it.

Assuming as he does that sentences and their constituents are ordered and grouped prior to the application of coordinative reductions, and noting that when the remaining verb is a left member of its predicate, the verb is absent from the right conjoined sentence, and vice versa, Ross proposes that the governing relationship be formulated as a general directionality condition on the application of a postulated verb-deletion, or gapping, transformation. He expresses this as a hypothesis to the effect that "The order in which *Gapping* operates depends on the order of elements at the time that the rule applies; if the identical elements are on left branches, *Gapping* operates forward; if they are on right branches, it operates backward" (1970:251). This condition would thus correctly predict the possible verbal reductions of English and Japanese from their respective unreduced coordinations: (A slash mark over a symbol stands here and throughout for the identity deletion of the constituent so marked.)

(5)	*English:*	(S (V O)) and (S (V̸ O))
	Japanese:	(S (O V̸)) and (S (O V))

For these languages, the directionality condition clearly would apply to all other ordinary coordination reductions as well. Thus, for example, the correct form of reduction with deleted subjects, objects, predicates, etc., can be derived from appropriate superficially unreduced paraphrases by application of a single, general directionality condition on deletion, a condition which allows for the identity deletion of any non-initial instance of a left member of a coordinated construction and of any non-final instance of a right member of such a construction. Thus, in English, for example, this directionality condition would not only account for the correct form of verbally-reduced coordinations such as

(6) (S (VO) and (S (V̸O)): (Nicholas (drank water)) and (Alexander (d̸r̸a̸n̸k vodka))),

but also for a large number of other types of reduced coordinations as well:

(7) (a) (S PRED) and (S̸ PRED): (Nicholas (drank water)) and (N̸i̸c̸h̸o̸l̸a̸s̸ (poured vodka))
    (b) (S (VØ)) and (S (VO)): (Nicholas (poured v̸o̸d̸k̸a̸)) and (Alexander (drank vodka))
    (c) (DET N) and (D̸E̸T̸ N): (The king) and (t̸h̸e̸ queen) are similar
    (d) (ADJ N) and (A̸D̸J̸ N): The (old men) and (o̸l̸d̸ women) danced
    (e) (ADJ N̸) and (ADJ N): The (young m̸e̸n̸) and (old men) danced

Although the above formulation of the directionality condition might not be entirely correct, and although its proper application requires the observance of certain other constraints on cyclic deletion and precedence ordering,[3] I know of no clear cases of

---

[3] Thus, for example, the identical adjectives of (a) may undergo reduction while those of (b) may not:

(a) Some big dogs and b̸i̸g̸ cats are running around
(b) Some big dogs and some big cats are running around
   *Some big dogs and some b̸i̸g̸ cats are running around
   *Some b̸i̸g̸ dogs and some big cats are running around

coordinative reduction which violate this condition in any English-
or Japanese-type language. Thus, regardless of how coordinative
reduction is ultimately accounted for, there is an observed FACT
about natural languages here which must be accounted for in some
way by any adequate linguistic theory. To distinguish this fact
from any particular hypotheses about the WAY in which coordinative reductions are derived, let us express it now in the form of the
following DIRECTIONALITY RELATION between reduced and unreduced coordinations:

(8)   There is a non-null set of natural languages L, such that
      for any language in L if
      (i)   ... A B ... and ... A B ...
      is a grammatical coordination in the language, then neither
      of the following coordinations is grammatical in that
      language:
      (ii)   *... B ... and ... A B ...
      (iii) *... A B ... and ... A ...

This ordering relation does not hold for Russian- and Hindi-type

---

That this is not simply a restriction to the effect that only the highest identical
constituent may be deleted is evidenced by the fact that even when this condition is unequivocally satisfied, as in (c), the identical adjectives are still not
reducible:
   (c)   Five big dogs and seven big cats are running around.
Similar hierarchical restrictions on reduction have been noted by Tai (1969) for
Mandarin Chinese. The nature and proposed explanation of such restrictions in
these and other languages have been discussed at some length in Koutsoudas
(1971) and Sanders and Tai (1972). In all these cases what appears to be opera-
tive are certain general (but language-variable) restrictions on the distance, in
terms of intervening construction bracketings, between the two operant terms of
any deletion transformation. These in turn might ultimately be reducible to a set
of still more general constraints on the scope of all grammatical processes or
relations. In any event, it will be necessary in any adequate treatment of reduction to account both for polylingual restrictions, like those shown in (b), and
for certain important differences between languages in respect to reduction,
e.g. the fact that in structures of the form SVO & SVO neither an identical V
nor an identical O is deletable in Mandarin, while both of these alternatives are
available in English:
   (d)   (a) John hit the dog and Bill h̶i̶t̶ the cat
         (b) John hit t̶h̶e̶ d̶o̶g̶ and Bill kicked the dog.
For further discussion, see Sanders and Tai (1972).

languages, since these have both unreduced coordinations of the form (SOV and SOV) and reductions of the form (SOV and SO), the latter being excluded by (iii) of the directionality relation for English- and Japanese-types. The Russian- and Hindi-type reductions thus constitute the major explanatory problem dealt with by Ross, and it is only in seeking a solution to this problem that any questions concerning the utility of reordering are relevant. Before turning to this matter, however, it is important to note two things about Ross's proposed treatment of verb-deletion as applied to the simpler case of English- and Japanese-type languages.

First, for these languages, Ross's verb deletion transformation and its associated directionality condition are applicable to SURFACE ORDERINGS of the constituents of SURFACE CONSTRUCTIONS. Thus there are ordinary gapping-type reductions of conjoined passive as well as active sentences in English, e.g.

(9)   (Water (was-drunk by-Nicholas)) and (vodka (w̶a̶s̶-̶d̶r̶u̶n̶k̶ by-Alexander)),

where the S and O of the English gapping schema (S(VO)) and (S(V̶O)) are underlying patients and agents, respectively. Similarly, there are gappings where O is an adverbial constituent,

(10)   (a)   (Nicholas (disappeared on-Monday) and Alexander (d̶i̶s̶a̶p̶p̶e̶a̶r̶e̶d̶ on-Thursday))
        (b)   (Nicholas (spoke cunningly) and Alexander (s̶p̶o̶k̶e̶ loudly),

and where S can be any oblique or non-oblique constituent that can occur as a superficial subject, e.g. a dative (11 a), an instrumental (11 b), or a locative (11 c):

(11)   (a)   (Nicholas (was-offered wine)) and (Alexander (w̶a̶s̶-̶o̶f̶f̶e̶r̶e̶d̶ vodka)) (cf. Someone offered wine *to* Nicholas)
        (b)   (This key (will-open the door)) and (that one (w̶i̶l̶l̶-̶o̶p̶e̶n̶ the trunk)) (cf. The door can be opened *with* this key)
        (c)   (Colorado (has nice-mountains)) and (Minnesota (h̶a̶s̶ nice-lakes)) (cf. There are nice mountains *in* Colorado)

It is evident, in fact, that for English- and Japanese-type languages at least, ALL coordination reductions are applicable to the surface ordering of constituents. Thus wherever there are alternate orderings of the same constituents, as in

(12) (a) Nicholas drank vodka
     (b) Vodka was drunk by Nicholas
(13) (a) John is interested in butterflies
     (b) Butterflies interest John
     (c) Butterflies are interesting to John
(14) (a) I like rice well-cooked
     (b) I like well-cooked rice[4]

there are various alternate coordination reductions, each standing in the general directionality relation with respect to its corresponding unreduced alternant:

(15) (a) Nicholas d̸r̸a̸n̸k̸ v̸o̸d̸k̸a̸ and Alexander drank vodka
         Nicholas drank vodka and N̸i̸c̸h̸o̸l̸a̸s̸ poured vodka
     (b) Vodka was drunk by Nicholas and v̸o̸d̸k̸a̸ w̸a̸s̸ d̸r̸u̸n̸k̸ b̸y̸ Alexander
         Vodka was drunk b̸y̸ N̸i̸c̸h̸o̸l̸a̸s̸ and v̸o̸d̸k̸a̸ w̸a̸s̸ poured by Nicholas
(16) (a) John is interested in b̸u̸t̸t̸e̸r̸f̸l̸i̸e̸s̸ and J̸o̸h̸n̸ has often been haunted by butterflies
     (b) Butterflies interest John and b̸u̸t̸t̸e̸r̸f̸l̸i̸e̸s̸ are hunted by Bill
     (c) Butterflies a̸r̸e̸ i̸n̸t̸e̸r̸e̸s̸t̸i̸n̸g̸ t̸o̸ J̸o̸h̸n̸ and moths are interesting to John
(17) (a) I like rice well-cooked and r̸i̸c̸e̸ well-seasoned
         I like rice w̸e̸l̸l̸-̸c̸o̸o̸k̸e̸d̸ and beans well-cooked
     (b) I like well-cooked r̸i̸c̸e̸ and well-seasoned rice
         I like well-cooked rice and w̸e̸l̸l̸-̸c̸o̸o̸k̸e̸d̸ beans

---

[4] No synonymy claims are implied by the grouping of sentences in (12-14); with respect to coordinative reduction it clearly makes no difference at all whether the members of each group are actually derived from a single underlying structure or not.

(a') *I like ~~rice~~ well-cooked and rice well-seasoned
   *I like rice well-cooked and beans ~~well-cooked~~
(b') *I like well-cooked rice and well-seasoned ~~rice~~[5]
   *I like ~~well-cooked~~ rice and well-cooked beans

It can readily be seen from examples such as these that if coordination reduction operates on ordered structures then all grammatical surface orderings in the language must be available for such operation and no reordering of constituents needs to be specified subsequent to it. Moreover, as evidenced by (17), and various other data such as

(18)   (a)   John wrote a letter to the president, and Bill to the governor
       (b)   *John wrote the president a letter, and Bill to the governor
(19)   (a)   John chased the dog, and Bill the cat
       (b)   *The dog was chased by John, and Bill the cat,

coordinative reduction, if it applies to ordered structures, not only CAN apply to surface orders alone, but in some cases at least, MUST apply only to such orders. Thus, assuming the conventional treatment of passivization in English by means of a reordering transformation, this transformation must be prevented from applying after the application of coordinative reduction in any derivation. The fact that hypothetical movement rules such as Passive must be prevented from applying subsequently to gapping and other coordinative reductions also demonstrates of course that coordinative reduction cannot be a pre-cyclic or pre-transformational process of any sort. This is also independently demonstrated by the entirely regular applicability of the general reduction processes to structures with numerically unbounded separations between logical predicates and their arguments, structures which can thus be generated ONLY by rules with the power of grammatical transformations. Thus, for example, in sentences such as

[5] This sentence appears to be somewhat less deviant than the others in (17 a'-b'), probably because of its resemblance to certain well-known archaic expressions such as *good men and true* as well as to such fully-grammatical non-adjectival pronominally-reduced phrases as *this rice and that* or *my rice*

(20) (a) Nicholas was believed to have drunk wine and
Alexander ~~was believed to have drunk~~ water

(b) Nicholas was believed to have drunk wine and
~~Nicholas was believed~~ to have been assassinated by
the rebels

(c) Could the fermentation of the wine have been considered to have been the cause of Nicholas' death and
~~could the fermentation of the wine have been considered to have been~~ the reason why Alexander
jumped out of the open window

it is clear that reduction can be appropriately effected only after the
application of various adjunction, deletion, and regrouping transformations to underlying structures which are radically different
in their constituency and grouping properties from the structures
which are ultimately reduced.

The fact that any coordinative reduction of ordered structures
must be effected subsequently to all syntactic structure-affecting
transformations in English clearly falsifies Ross's hypothesis that
"*gapping* is an anywhere rule in any language in whose grammar it
appears" (Ross 1970: 259). For if gapping were an "anywhere"
rule in English — that is, a rule that can apply at any point in a
derivation at which its structural description is satisfied — it would
be applicable either before or after the application of Passive. But
this would allow for incorrect derivations such as

(21) Nicholas drank wine, and Alexander drank vodka
—Gapping→
Nicholas drank wine, and Alexander vodka —Passive→
*Wine was drunk by Nicholas, and Alexander vodka

in precisely those cases where Gapping is applied before Passive.[6]

---

and yours (cf. *my rice and your*). It will also be observed that asterisks are used
here and throughout to signify not only absolute ungrammaticality but also
ungrammaticality relative to a given meaning or paraphrase set.

[6] Parallel evidence exists for all other types of passive or quasi-passive alternation sets. Cf., for example,

Caesar was interested in empires and Cleopatra in emperors
*Empires were interesting to Caesar, and Cleopatra in emperors.

Thus if Passive is a rule of English, then Gapping cannot be an anywhere rule in English. And, if gapping is a rule or sub-rule of any language, it is certainly a rule or sub-rule of English; it follows then that gapping cannot be an anywhere rule in all grammars in which it occurs. The evidence from English- and Japanese-type languages, in fact, strongly suggests an entirely different hypothesis: namely, that all coordinative reduction (including gapping) applies universally to surface structures subsequent to the application of all other syntactic transformations.[7]

It should be noted that Ross's hypothesis about the ordering of gapping operations cannot be saved by any appeal to "across the board" conditions on rule application of the sort discussed in Ross (1967). Thus, even if it could be shown that some facts can be

---

If there are cyclic rules, however, and if every reordering rule is cyclic, it might be possible, by means of an *ad hoc* cyclic reduction constraint, to assure that the reorderings can only apply before reduction of any coordinate set of simple sentences. Many non-cyclic reorderings have been proposed in the literature, however, such as Topicalization, WH-Movement, and Ross's own rule of Scrambling (Ross 1967).

[7] Aside from processes of an obviously lexical or phonological character it appears that the only rules which must necessarily follow the application of coordinative reduction are rules which specify the proper extraposition, ordering, and agreement properties of affixes. The subsequence of these essentially intralexical processes to coordinative reduction is necessitated by the fact that concord relations differ depending on whether or not coordinative reduction has applied,

    (a) A dog was running around *and a cat was running around*
    (b) *A dog was running around *and a cat were running around*
    (c) *A dog *and a cat was running around*
    (d) A dog *and a cat were running around,*

and by the fact that affixes (as opposed to clitics and other non-sublexical constituents) can never undergo identity deletion:

    (a)   I like to sing and t∅ dance
    (b) *I like sing-i̸n̸g̸ and dance-ing
    (c)   The boy'ś and the girl's horse is running around
    (d) *The boyś and the girls are running around.

Since there are clearly no non-phonological rules which depend on the prior extraposition or concord-marking of inflectional affixes, these intralexical processes could apply post-syntactically, where ordered coordination reduction is the last post-cyclic syntactic process.

accounted for only if it is assumed that some transformations apply only on an all or none basis to the conjuncts of any coordination, it is clear that no optional reordering rule like Passive can be such a transformation. Thus the differential application or non-application of passivization has no effect whatever on the grammaticality of unreduced coordinations such as

(22)   Nicholas drank wine, and vodka was drunk by Alexander

or post-Passive reductions such as

(23)   Nicholas drank wine and N̸i̸c̸h̸o̸l̸a̸s̸ was assassinated by
         by Alexander.

In the latter case, in fact, it is clearly necessary that Passive NOT be restricted to across-the-board application, and that it be permitted to apply BEFORE coordination reduction. It would thus be possible to preserve the notion of a cyclic or anywhere reduction process only by the imposition of entirely *ad hoc* and unnatural restrictions on Passive and all other rules effecting the reordering of constituents. These restrictions would have to exclude application within a sentence which is a conjunct of a coordination which has already undergone reduction, even if the reduction has had no effect upon that sentence itself. Aside from the patently unnatural character of such a rule-condition, Ross's gapping theory would also need to account for the fact that his proposed "scrambling" rule for Russian and Hindi does NOT require this condition, in spite of its being a movement rule of fundamentally the same character apparently as Passive and other movement rules of English and Japanese. In fact, since Ross's treatment of Russian and Hindi gapping depends in a crucial way on the assumption that a movement rule (scrambling) may apply after a reduction, while all the evidence from English and Japanese suggests that this must never be permitted,[8]

---

[8]   Some apparent violations of this constraint, however, appear to be less objectionable than others. Thus, for example, when the unreduced constituents of a reduction are temporal and locative adverbials, as in

(a)   Tomorrow I will go to London, and next week I̸ w̸i̸l̸l̸ g̸o̸ to Paris
(b)   I will go to London tomorrow, and I̸ w̸i̸l̸l̸ g̸o̸ to Paris next week,

there is also a third alternant which is nearly as acceptable as these,

we are led naturally to conclude either that the reduction processes of different languages are radically different, or, much more plausibly, that Ross's account of Russian and Hindi gapping is not correct, and that in these languages too all coordinative reductions apply solely with respect to the superficial orderings or groupings of syntactic constituents.[9]

In short, then, the facts about gapping and other forms of coordinative reduction in English- and Japanese-type languages provide no evidence in support of either axiomatic or variant ordering. On the contrary, these facts are strongly suggestive of the hypothesis that the only order of constituents which is gram-

----

(a′) I will go to London tomorrow, and next week to Paris,

while a fourth logically-possible alternant, which is related to (b) in apparently the same way as (a′) is related to (a), is clearly much more seriously deviant:

(b′) *Tomorrow I will go to London, and to Paris next week.

I am unable to suggest any explanation for gradations of this sort, nor for a number of closely related facts about adverbial alternations in such reductions as

(a) Today we have Kokomo, and tomorrow w̶e̶ h̶a̶v̶e̶ the whole world
(b) We have Kokomo today, and w̶e̶ h̶a̶v̶e̶ the whole world tomorrow

(a′) We have Kokomo today, and tomorrow the whole world
(b′) ?Today we have Kokomo, and the whole world tomorrow.

[9] The matter of "across the board" constraints will be raised again subsequently with respect to the application or ordering rules. I know of no valid arguments for the necessity of any such constraint on the application of any optional transformation or any rule which is not either a phonological rule, a lexical rule, or an ordering rule — all of the latter being not only obligatory but also essentially post-syntactic. Ross has proposed that Gapping (1970) and Relative Movement (1967) be specifically marked as "across the board" rules, but these proposals are empirically unmotivated; any derivation which can be effected by across-the-board Gapping can also be effected without loss of generality by means of repeated pairwise applications of a simple binary Gapping rule defined on adjacent structures; as for Relative Movement, since there is no motivation whatever for assuming that Coordinative Reduction precedes any relativization process (see Postal 1971), or for assuming that there are any subordinate sentential coordinations prior to the application of Coordination Reduction (this is true even for grammars which postulate axiomatic structures of the form [NP [NP & S]] in addition to initial structures of the form $[\#S\#]^n$), it can always be the case that a relativization process will apply only with respect to a unary head and a unary sentential attribute, the question of across-the-board applicability thus never arising at all.

matically significant is their surface order, and that this order is relevant only to post-cyclic grammatical processes.[10] Thus, for these languages, Ross's treatment of gapping as a deletion operation on ordered structures governed by the general directionality condition is entirely compatible, apparently, with the hypothesis that both ordering and coordination reduction are post-cyclic processes with all cyclic and pre-cyclic rules applying to unordered structures. In other words, the evidence thus far is compatible with the following schema for the derivation of sentences in English- and Japanese-type languages:

(22) UNORDERED AXIOMATIC STRUCTURES
|

| Syntactic Transformations |
| Applying to Unordered Structures |

↓

UNORDERED SURFACE STRUCTURES
|

| Post-Cyclic Ordering Rules |

↓

ORDERED SURFACE STRUCTURES
|

| Coordination Reduction |

↓

REDUCED ORDERED SURFACE STRUCTURES
|

| Lexical and Phonological Rules |

↓

ORDERED PHONETIC REPRESENTATIONS

[10] The terms "cyclic", "pre-cyclic", and "post-cyclic" will generally be used here to refer to the general types of facts and relations which have traditionally been accounted for by means of rules categorized according to these terms. Use of these terms is thus not intended to imply either acceptance or rejection of the claim that any rules are either extrinsically or intrinsically ordered in any or all of these ways. A more precise, though excessively cumbersome, way of expressing what is usually intended here by the term "cyclic" would be "ordinary

We will argue shortly that coordinative reduction applies before rather than after ordering, and that there are thus apparently no syntactic processes at all which depend on the prior specification of the order of any constituents. It is important to note here, though, that even if this argument could be shown to be false, that is, even if it could be shown that reduction MUST apply to ordered structures, it would still be the case for English- and Japanese-type languages at least that only a demonstrably post-cyclic process would be dependent upon prior ordering and thus that ordering itself can be specified post-cyclically.

The second major observation about Ross's treatment of gapping in English and Japanese concerns the obviously central matter of explanation. Thus the task of the linguist here is not simply to enumerate the grammatical reductions in these languages and to note that each of these reductions constitutes an instance of the general directionality relation. The primary task, rather, is to discover the general grammatical principles which DETERMINE grammatical reductions in these languages and to explain WHY the directionality relation does, in fact, hold with respect to this class of objects.

If it is assumed, as Ross does, that coordinative reduction applies with respect to ordered structures, then the existence of the directionality relation in surface structures could be accounted for either by requiring observance of the directionality relation as a condition on the reduction rule itself, which is what Ross proposes, or by specifying the observance of this relation as a necessary condition for the acceptability of surface structures, in which case the reduction rule would be freed of all directionality restrictions.[11]

(post-axiomatic, pre-lexical) syntactic process", i.e. a process specified typically by means of identity deletion, iteration, or grouping transformations applied to non-superficial representations of linguistic objects.

[11] The output condition alternative, however, raises a serious problem which is possibly inherently unsolvable in the context of ordered-base grammar. Thus if syntactic transformations can apply only to ordered strings, there is simply no way to formulate a simple unconditional deletion transformation, one which merely deletes one of two identical constituents. Therefore, even if the directionality condition is expressed as an output condition, it appears that TWO

For the mere enumeration of grammatical reductions, these two alternatives are equally adequate; the only criterion for choosing between them would thus have to be a metatheoretical one: either the universal exclusion of surface acceptability conditions (which appears to be empirically impossible; see, e.g. Perlmutter [1968]), or the universal exclusion of conditions on specific rules (which seems empirically quite possible and obviously most desirable), or, conceivably, the differential weighting of surface-conditions and rule-conditions according to some general metric for the evaluation of alternative grammars.

---

gapping rules would still be required, one to delete an antecedent constituent of an identity pair, the other to delete a subsequent constituent of such a pair. Although these rules could be conflated by a mirror image convention, there would be no reason then not to incorporate the directionality condition into this conflation too. In short, there appears to be no motivated way to prevent ordered-string transformations from at least partially duplicating the functions of any proposed well-formedness condition on surface structures. Essentially the same problem arises with respect to Perlmutter's proposed output-condition treatment of the ordering of clitic pronouns in Spanish (Perlmutter 1968: Chapter 4). This problem, which Perlmutter discusses but does not attempt to solve, stems from the fact that an output condition can be justified here only if clitics are allowed to become attached to verbs in a RANDOM order, since otherwise there would be an overlap in the order-characterization functions of the output condition and the attachment transformation. Although it is possible to formulate ordered-string rules which effect random orderings, e.g.,

     CLITIC ATTACHMENT (Obligatory, Mirror-Image)
     X & [PRO, -STRESS] & Y & [Z & W] & U
                    V
     1   2   3   4   5   6 → 1 Ø 3 4 2 5 6

these formulations are excessively complex, not only with respect to our intuitive understanding of the notion of simple (order-irrelevant) inclusion, but also relative to similar rules which effect a proper NON-RANDOM ordering to begin with. It should be noted, incidentally, that while all of the ORDERING functions of Perlmutter's surface-structure conditions can be achieved with equal or greater generality by means of ordering rules, Perlmutter's conditions also account for the ill-formedness of certain structures which include improper GROUPINGS of constituents and thus where the structure is ungrammatical no matter HOW the constituents are ordered. If such restrictions cannot be accounted for as consequences of anaphora formation or other general grammatical processes, output conditions would still be required then even if all of their order-characterization functions are eliminated in favor of general ordering rules. (But see Ch. 4 for discussion of the Compatibility of Products Constraint, which might effect a blocking of an ordering rule precisely in such cases as these.)

Both of these alternatives are devoid of explanatory value here, however, since they fail to contribute anything towards the explanation of the central fact that the directionality relation does hold for all grammatical reductions in English and Japanese. To explain this fact it would be necessary to show that it follows as a necessary consequence of certain independently-motivated grammatical principles. But both Ross's rule-condition treatment and the type of surface-condition alternative described above simply incorporate the fact as an entirely *ad hoc* principle of the theory that is supposed to explain it. We will show that there is, in fact, a very simple and natural explanation for the directionality relation in reduced coordinations, an explanation which follows from rules which are motivated entirely independently of the reduction process itself. First, though, let us summarize Ross's treatment of the remaining facts about verbal reduction in Russian- and Hindi-type languages.

The occurrence of reductions of both the English and the Japanese types in Russian and of the Japanese type in Hindi raises no additional explanatory problems, since Russian has unreduced clauses both of the form SVO (as in English) and of the form SOV (as in Japanese) while Hindi has unreduced clauses only of the latter form. Thus these reductions can be accounted for just like those of English and Japanese by the application of the same directionally-restricted reduction rule to the superficial structures of unreduced coordinations. Problems arise only with respect to the third type of reduction, SOV and SO, a pattern which occurs in both Russian and Hindi and which violates the superficial directionality relation that holds for all the other patterns of reduction in all languages.

To account for this superficially anomalous pattern without abandoning the general formulation of reduction that is adequate for the derivation of the other patterns, Ross proposes the following additional hypotheses:[12] (1) that prior to the application of any

---

[12]   I have emended Ross's formulation of some of these hypotheses in the hope of making them somewhat more explicit and more compatible with various related facts not dealt with in Ross's study. The actual formulations Ross gives are as follows: (1) "Thus we can see that one long chain of inference in necessary to

reductive processes the order of clause constituents is SVO in languages like English, Russian, and Hindi, and SOV in languages like Japanese; (2) that there is, for languages like Russian, an optional reordering rule effecting the postposition of verbs in clauses; (3) that whenever this reordering rule is applicable, gapping is applicable either before or after it; (4) that the reordering rule, which Ross calls SCRAMBLING, can apply no more than once in the derivation of any given clause; and (5) that there is, for languages like Hindi, an additional verb postposing rule which applies obligatorily either before or after the optional application of gapping.

There are a number of questions that could be raised concerning

establish that Russian has the deep structure order SVO, and not SOV" (p. 253). "[Japanese-type] languages, which gap only backward, have SOV order in deep structure, whereas ... [Hindi-type] languages, which gap in both directions, have underlying SVO order .... I would argue that in Hindi, verbs start out before their objects ..." (p. 257) "Type II languages, like English, exhibit SVO order" (p. 249); (2) "... *Scrambling*, the rule which optionally permutes major elements of a clause, subject to various conditions which need not concern us here" (pp. 251-252); (3) "If we assume ... that *Gapping* is an "anywhere rule" — i.e., a rule that can apply at any point in a derivation (p. 252) ... For if *Gapping* is an anywhere rule, it will be able to apply before and after *Scrambling* ..." (p. 253) "*Gapping* is an anywhere rule in any language in whose grammar it appears" (p. 259); (4) "But then, if backward gapping occurs after *Scrambling*, the last conjunct will remain in the SOV order of sentence (10b), not the SVO of (14), for Scrambling has been passed in the ordering, and cannot reapply" (p. 253); (5) "... I would argue that in Hindi, verbs start out before their object, and then, after *Gapping* has had a chance to apply forward, they are obligatorily moved to the end of their VP, where backward gapping will subsequently also be able to apply" (p. 257).

I will not comment on these formulations, except to note that if any languages have passive or quasi-passive transformations which regroup and/or reorder the constituents of deep-structure clauses, then Gapping obviously cannot be an "anywhere" rule — except perhaps within some post-cyclic and fundamentally post-syntactic component, which might possibly also include a Scrambling rule. Similarly, since Gapping and other reductions can always apply with respect to the SUPERFICIAL subjects, verbs, and complements of clauses, IN-DEPENDENTLY OF their constituency and/or ordering in deep structure all references to "underlying order" and "order in deep structure" in Ross's paper must presumably be interpreted as really referring only to "superficial or nearly-superficial order" or "order in post-cyclic or post-syntactic structure". Ross's discussion and conclusions thus imply nothing whatever about the ordering or non-ordering of elements in deep structures.

the explanatory value of each of these hypotheses. Thus, for example, Ross provides no independent motivation for either of the proposed reordering rules, nor indeed for any of the other hypotheses. The Hindi reordering rule is especially questionable, of course, since it is functionally identical to the other reordering rule and differs only in being obligatory rather than optional; even if the Hindi rule were replaced by an output condition, moreover, this patently *ad hoc* feature of the theory apparently cannot be eliminated except by eliminating the theory itself. The same is true with respect to the peculiar rule-specific conditions that are imposed with respect to the relative order of application of the various proposed rules; although there is no reason to believe that *ad hoc* restrictions of this sort would ever be required for the principled description of any other linguistic phenomena, these exceedingly powerful devices play an essential role here.

If we suspend judgement on the empirical motivation and metatheoretical acceptability of these hypotheses, though, we find that Ross's theory does adequately account for the occurrence of the four observed patterns of verbally-reduced coordinations:

(23)
English: ORDERING →SVO and SVO—GAPPING →*SVO and SO*
Japanese: ORDERING →SOV and SOV—GAPPING →*SO and SOV*
Russian: ORDERING →SVO and SVO—GAPPING →*SVO and SO*
                              | |
                    SCRAMBLING   SCRAMBLING (opt)
                              | ↓
                              ↓   *SOV and SO*
                    SOV and SOV—GAPPING →*SO and SOV*
Hindi: ORDERING →SVO and SVO—GAPPING →SVO and SO
                              | |
                    HINDI SCRAMBLE   HINDI SCRAMBLE (obl)
                              | ↓
                              ↓   *SOV and SO*
                    SOV and SOV—GAPPING →*SO and SOV*

Thus regardless of the various questionable properties of this theory, and regardless of the fact that it still fails to provide any explanation of the directionality restriction itself, the theory does correctly account for certain significant facts and it does this by making essential use of reordering rules effecting derivations which

violate the Invariant Order Constraint. If this constraint is correct, then Ross's theory is not a possible theory about natural languages. To justifiably maintain the correctness of the Invariant Order Constraint, then, it would be necessary to show that all of the facts accounted for by Ross's theory can be accounted for with equal or greater generality by some theory which observes the Invariant Order Constraint. This will now be shown.

Let us consider the facts about verbal reduction then in terms of a theory of grammar which requires order-free underlying structures and the derivation of all superficial orderings by general ordering rules in accordance with the invariant order condition.

We will assume then that the simple non-subordinate clauses of all languages are analyzable as

(24) $[S, [V, O]]$

at some derivational stage prior to the application of any ordering rule. (It should be recalled that $[A, B]$ and $[B, A]$ are alternate notations representing exactly the same structure, and that $[A, [B, C]]$ and $[[A, B], C]$ represent distinctively different structures. The symbols S, V, and O are used here, as previously, to stand for whatever elements or bracketings distinctively characterize all superficial subjects, verbs, and objects or complements, respectively.)

The correct order of clause constituents in English- and Japanese-type languages can be accounted for by the ordering rules

(25) (1a) $[V, O] \rightarrow [V \& O]$ (Objects are ordered after Verbs)
     (1b) $[V, O] \rightarrow [O \& V]$ (Objects are ordered before Verbs)
     (2) $[S, O] \rightarrow [S \& O]$ (Subjects are ordered before Objects)

where (1a) and (2) are included in the grammar of English and (1b) and (2) are included in the grammar of Japanese. Thus, the application of these rules to any structure of the form (24), say, the structure represented by

(26) $[Cleopatra, [admired, Caesar]]$,

will correctly derive the superficial ordering of its constituents:

(27) *English*: [Cleopatra,   [admired,   Caesar]]—Rule 1a →
                [Cleopatra,   [admired & Caesar]]—Rule 2 →
                [Cleopatra & [admired & Caesar]]
     Japanese: [Cleopatra,   [admired,   Caesar]]—Rule 1b →
                 [Cleopatra,   [Caesar & admired]]—Rule 2 →
                 [Cleopatra & [Caesar & admired]].

These ordering transformations operate in a very straightforward and general way, mapping each of an infinite set of unordered constituent sets into a unique ordered constituent set, with the grouping of constituents remaining invariant under transformation. Because of the latter restriction, ordering rules are effectively limited to the ordering of immediate constituents of the same construction; a rule such as (2), for example, can apply only to an intersection of A and B, where A includes S and B includes O, and where A and B are sister constituents included in exactly the same set of parenthesizations; thus, while Rule (2) explicitly specifies a generalization about the relative order of superficial subjects and objects, it actually effects, in all complete clauses, the ordering of the superficial subject and its entire predicate.

Given the presently-proposed metatheory, these ordering rules perform the necessary function of deriving the correct ordering of all clause-constituents from their axiomatically-unordered superficial groupings. They thus provide an entirely principled and natural expression of certain empirically-significant generalizations which cannot be expressed at all by any grammar that accepts axiomatically-ordered underlying structures; namely, that in English and Japanese ALL superficial subjects are ordered before superficial objects REGARDLESS OF whether these are derived from underlying agents, patients, datives, or whatever, and all superficial objects are ordered after verbs in English and before verbs in Japanese, again REGARDLESS OF their derivational sources.

Moreover, when we compare the order of constituents in the simple clauses of these languages with that in their respective verbally-reduced coordinations,

(28) *English*: [S & [V & O]]: [[S & [V & O]] & [S & O]]
        Japanese: [S & [O & V]]: [[S & O] & [S & [O & V]]],

it is immediately evident that the generalizations about the ordering
of clause constituents expressed by rules (25) are equally true of
both the clausal and sub-clausal constituents of reduced coordinations of the same language. Thus, in English, constituents
including verbs, [V] or [S, [V, O]] always precede sister constituents
including objects, [O] or [S, O], while in Japanese the reverse is
always true. Similarly, for both languages, superficial subject
constituents always precede object constituents both in simple
clauses and in all reduced coordinations. It is clear then that in
order to account for the facts about the ordering of superficial
clause constituents in a maximally simple and general way it is
necessary that the ordering rules (25) be permitted to apply to the
constituents of reduced coordinations as well as to those of unreduced simple clauses. This is possible, however, only if coordination reduction is logically prior to ordering in phonetically-directed
derivations — that is, only if reduction processes apply to unordered structures with the products of reduction subsequently
undergoing the same general ordering processes as are undergone
by all unreduced clause structures.

It is thus necessary to assume that, for English- and Japanese-
type languages at least, coordinative reduction applies as an
identity deletion to structures of the form

(29) [[S, [V, O]], [S, [V, O]]].

In the case of verbal identity, the general reduction process will
effect the derivation from (29) of verbal reductions, or gappings,
of the form

(30) [[S, [V, O]], [S, O]].

These latter structures satisfy the structural description of the
independently-motivated general ordering rules for superficial
constituents; their superficial ordering can thus be specified by these
rules in an entirely regular way:

(31) *English*: [S, [V, O]], [S, O]   (given)
                  [S, [V, O]] & [S, O]   (25.1a)
                  [S, [V & O]] & [S, O]   (25.1a)
                  [S & [V & O]] & [S & O]   (25.2)
      Japanese: [S, [V, O]], [S, O]   (given)
                  [S, O] & [S, [V, O]]   (25.1b)
                  [S, O] & [S, [O & V]]   (25.1b)
                  [S & O] & [S & [O & V]]   (25.2)

By assuming that constituents are axiomatically unordered and
that coordinative reduction precedes the ordering of clause constituents, we can thus account for the ordering properties of reduced
coordinations entirely by means of general rules which would be
necessary even if coordinations and coordinative reductions did not
exist. This treatment, in other words, provides an EXPLANATION
of the directionality relation that holds with respect to reduced
coordinations in English and Japanese, since observance of this
relation now follows as a necessary consequence of general rules
which are entirely independent of any specific facts about coordinative reduction. As shown above, no explanation of the
directionality relation can be provided by any grammar which
assumes that reduction applies to ordered rather than unordered
structures, since for any such grammar the directionality relation
itself must be incorporated as an *ad hoc* statement of the grammar
itself, either as a condition on the application of reductions, as in
Ross's treatment, or as a condition on the well-formedness of
surface structures. Thus, since the directionality relation is an
empirically-significant fact about English- and Japanese-type languages, being neither logically necessary nor following as a necessary consequence of any independently motivated metatheoretical
constraint on grammars, we have here a clear instance of the
explanatory inadequacy of the metatheoretical assumption of
axiomatic ordering relative to the assumption that all underlying
structures are unordered. Moreover, since the explanation of the
directionality relation evidently depends also on the phonetically-
directed derivational precedence of reduction over ordering, this

evidence provides further support for the even stronger meta-theoretical constraint of invariant derivational ordering. For, if it is true as argued above that coordinative reduction is necessarily a post-cyclic process — or, more relevantly, that it must at least follow in phonetically-directed derivations all rules which affect the determination of superficial subjects and objects — then, since reduction must precede ordering, it follows that all cyclic and pre-cyclic rules affecting superficial constituency must apply to un-ordered structures. Thus if no syntactic rules depend on the order of constituents, there can clearly be no reason whatever for allow-ing more than one ordering of the constituents of any structure in any derivation.

The assumption that reduction precedes ordering not only leads to a principled and entirely natural explanation of the directionality relation in reduced coordinations, but also allows for a formulation of the coordinative reduction rule itself which is considerably more general and more metatheoretically defensible than any formula-tion which applies with respect to ordered structures. Thus if reduction were subsequent to ordering, it would have to effect the deletion of identical constituents which are either (a) leftmost in a clause, (b) rightmost in a clause, or, as in the case of gapping in the ordinary sense, (c) medial in a clause. An adequate reduction schema for English then would need to be a principled conflation of the sub-rules

(32) $_a[X \& Y]\,\&\,_a[X \& Z]$ (e.g. John sang and J̶o̶h̶n̶ danced)
       $_a[W \& X]\,\&\,_a[U \& X]$ (e.g. John s̶a̶n̶g̶ and Bill sang)
       $_a[W \&\,_b[X \& Y]]\,\&\,_a[U \&\,_b[X \& Z]]$ (e.g. John ate rice
                                                       and Bill a̶t̶e̶ fish),

where identical capital letters signify identical structures and where identical lower case letters signify generic identity of constructions. Such conflation is impossible, however, without the postulation of certain metatheoretically indefensible *ad hoc* conditions on the application of specific rules or else a somewhat more general mirror-image convention for rule application of the sort that has been proposed by E. Bach (1968) and R. Langacker (1969b). Even in the

latter case, however, the resulting conflation will be somewhat more complex and less revealing than the corresponding reduction rule for unordered structures.

Langacker and Bach have correctly observed that if all transformations apply to ordered structures there will be certain pairs of rules which are precisely identical except that the input and output terms of the two rules are in opposite orders, the rightmost term of the structural description of one rule being the leftmost term of the structural description of the other, etc. Since there is an evidently non-accidental relationship between the members of such pairs of mirror-image rules, a relationship which cannot be expressed in terms of any of the ordinary conventions for rule-conflation, Langacker and Bach propose that an additional conflation convention be adopted, whereby rules are marked as to whether or not they are mirror-image rules, with only one member of a mirror-image pair constituting an abbreviation for both members of the pair.[13] It is clear that if coordinative reduction applies to ordered structures it is a mirror-image rule in this sense.[14] Dis-

---

[13] As noted by Langacker (1969b), Bach's "neighborhood convention" is substantively identical in most cases to the mirror-image convention; for example, the neighborhood format, $A \rightarrow B/C$, and the mirror-image format, Mirror-Image: $CA \rightarrow CB$, are only notational variants expressing the conflation of exactly the same pair of substatements, $CA \rightarrow CB$ and $AC \rightarrow BC$. Although Langacker explicitly allows for the possibility of "partial" mirror-image conflation — a possibility which is not excluded in Bach's formulation either — all of Langacker's actual examples of partial conflations are either based on highly dubious substatements or else are readily reformulated as complete rather than partial mirror-image statements. In any event, for simplicity of discussion and on the basis of intuitive notions of rule-naturalness, I am assuming here that if there are mirror-image conflations at all they must necessarily conflate statements whose respective structural descriotions and output descriptions are COMPLETE mirror-images of each other, i.e. pairs of statements of the form

(a) $a_1 \ldots a_n \rightarrow b_1 \ldots b_n$
(b) $a_n \ldots a_1 \rightarrow b_n \ldots b_1$

For a general critical discussion of mirror-image rules in syntax and phonology, see Norman (1973).

[14] Langacker also has observed certain mirror-image properties in Ross's formulation of Conjunction Reduction (Ross 1967: 175) and Gapping (Ross 1970), and he proposes separate partial mirror-image conflations of each of

regarding presently irrelevant details, this rule could be formulated as follows:

(33) ORDERED REDUCTION (Optional, Mirror-Image)

$$_a[\ _a[W\ _b[X\ Y]]\ _a[U\ _b[X\ Z]]]$$
$$\begin{array}{ccccccc} 1 & 2 & 3 & 4 & 5 & 6 & \rightarrow \\ 1 & 2 & 3 & 4 & \emptyset & 6 & \end{array}$$

---

these formulations (Langacker 1969b: 585, 597), with underlining signifying that part of the conflation which represents a mirror-image pair of structures:

CONJUNCTION REDUCTION

$$[AND, [A, X]^n_s]_s$$
$$\begin{array}{ccc} 1 & \underline{2\ \ 3} & \rightarrow 2 \neq\ _s[1, \emptyset, 3]_s \end{array}$$

GAPPING

AND + X, NP, V, NP, NP, V, NP, Y
$$\begin{array}{ccccccccc} 1 & 2 & \underline{3} & 4 & 5 & \underline{6} & 7 & 8 & \rightarrow 1, 2, 3, 4, 5, \emptyset, 7, 8 \end{array}$$
Conditions: $3 = 6, 2 \neq 5$

On the irrelevance of connectives and plural applicability to the formulation of coordinative reduction, see Notes 1 and 9 of this chapter. Langacker presents no justification for the postulation of two separate rules for the optional reduction of coordinations, nor does he discuss any of the various problems of overlapping function which arise if multiple reduction rules are postulated, e.g. the problem that for languages like Japanese verbal reductions will be effected by means of both of Langacker's rules while each rule will assign a different constituent structure to the same input and the same output ordering of constituents. It is possible that Ross, Langacker, and others have treated Gapping separately from other reductive processes because they wish to incorporate in the rule for the latter but not the former a "node-raising" regrouping process of the sort proposed by Stanley Peters in his unpublished study of coordination. It has not yet been demonstrated that such regrouping is necessary; but more importantly, there is no reason to believe that it would NECESSARILY have to be specified CONCURRENTLY with reduction. Evidence of the independence of reduction and regrouping has in fact been presented by Tai (1969). See also Sanders (1972) and Ch. 4 of the present study. In any event, however, the correct specification of intonationally-significant boundaries apparently cannot be effected directly by EITHER of the two rules assumed by Langacker. (Cf. Ross 1970: 253-255.) Facts about intonation or superficial constituency thus cannot be used to support the assumption of multiple rules of coordination reduction. I can think of no other possible empirical support for this assumption either.

For well-formed verbal reductions Langacker's Gapping conditions must also include the condition $4 \neq 7$, since verbs are not deletable unless both subjects AND complements are not identical. This is evidently only a special case of a general hierarchical precedence relation with respect to coordinative reduction (cf. Koutsoudas 1971; Tai 1969), a relation which is implicitly assumed throughout here but which has no direct bearing on the particular points at issue.

Thus for the sub-rule directly represented, the identical constituents X are leftmost members of a construction, and the reduction is effected by the deletion of the subsequent instance of X. For the other sub-rule included in (33), which can be readily inspected if the page is held before a mirror or turned upside down, the parentheses labeled b will be the right rather than left boundaries of some construction, the identical constituents X will be the right-most rather than leftmost members of the construction, and the deleted X of term 5 will be the antecedent rather than subsequent instance of the identical constituent.

This rule would apparently provide an adequate and quite general means for the derivation of correct reductions from correctly ordered unreduced coordinations. Before any conflation convention can be legitimately incorporated into linguistic theory, however, it must be shown that at least one conflation governed by the convention is NECESSARY for the explanation of some significant linguistic data. This has not been shown for the mirror-image convention, nor, as far as I can determine, for any other categorial conflation convention for SYNTACTIC rules. It is evident, in fact, that the most widely-used of such conventions — those involving the union and disjunction of strings, associated with parenthesis and brace notations, respectively — typically OBSCURE significant generalizations — in the case of union by allowing terms to appear in a rule when their presence of absence has no bearing on the rule's applicability or derivational function, in the case of disjunction by failing to differentiate accidental assemblages (like a trout and a man breathing under water) from natural classes (like a trout and a goldfish breathing under water) whose members share common properties and jointly obey those rules which apply to the inter-section of those properties. The only empirical arguments for con-flation that I know of are those in Chomsky (1967), where it is shown that conjunctive and disjunctive conflation conventions allow for the determination of explanatorily useful orderings of related phonological rules, and in Kiparsky (1968), where it is argued that conflatability might serve to characterize those cases where two or more rules are simultaneously lost during the course

of language transmission. Neither of these arguments is very convincing, however, and neither provides evidence that predictions generated from conflations are not equally predictable from the formal relations between the rules that are conflated. It is possible that similar arguments might be brought to bear on the question of syntactic conflations, although with respect to the mirror-image convention this would obviously require that there be a non-arbitrary order of applicability among the members of any mirror-image pair.[15] Even if this could be shown to be true,

---

[15] Langacker does not discuss the matter of subrule ordering at all, and it appears that the order of subrule application is actually empirically non-significant in all of his own examples of mirror-image conflations. Bach has discussed subrule ordering with respect to mirror-image conflations of obligatory phonological rules (Bach 1968), although I find his argument for significant ordering unconvincing here. Thus, for example, Bach argues that in velar stop assimilation in English, the frontness or backness of a following vowel dominates over that of a preceding vowel in determining the frontness-backness of an intervocalic velar — and thus that the prevocalic subrule of velar assimilation to adjacent vowels must be applied before the postvocalic subrule. However, as far as I can determine for my own dialect at least, the position of an intervocalic velar represents a compromise between the assimilations dictated by positionally-different vowels and not a complete assimilation to either one of them. Thus for me the velar in *rocky* is articulated farther forward than the one in *rock* and also farther back than the one in *keep*; the same compromise or summation relation holds for the velar of *becalm* with respect to those of *beak* and *calm*. A more important consideration, however, is that when we deal with allophonic alternations of this sort, there are typically no general rules which depend essentially on the specification or non-specification of the given phonetic distinction. It is thus difficult to justify the inclusion of these rules in grammars rather than, say, theories of motor behavior. And, since the distinctions that are specified presumably play no role in the explanation of any other facts about the language, there is no LINGUISTIC way to demonstrate that these distinctions even exist, let alone to determine their precise characteristics and manner of determination. To demonstrate that there are significant orderings of phonological mirror-image rules, then, it will be necessary to find such evidence with respect to general rules of a morphophonemic rather than allophonic character. Bach's discussion of vowel harmony (1968: 143-147) appears to suggest that such evidence might be found if it is assumed that there is always some SINGLE SEGMENT whose inherent properties determine the harmonic properties of the morphemes or words which include it. There is an at least equally plausible assumption, however, to the effect that harmony is the product of a "downward" rather than "side-to-side" process whereby certain phonological elements which are axiomatic immediate constituents of a word or morpheme are distributed downward to certain of its

however, acceptance of the mirror-image convention with respect to some but not all rules would effectively block all efforts to explain WHY mirror-image relations hold in precisely those cases where they do hold.

Even if the mirror-image conflation convention is accepted, we still find that the ordered reduction rule (33) which it makes possible is less simple and less revealing than a reduction rule that applies to unordered structures. Thus, again disregarding irrelevant details, the reduction of unordered coordinate structures could be effected by a universal rule formulated as follows:

(34)   UNORDERED REDUCTION (Optional)
$$_a[\ _a[W, X],\ _a[U, X]]$$
$$1 \quad 2 \quad\quad 3 \quad 4 \ \rightarrow$$
$$1 \quad 2 \quad\quad 3 \quad \emptyset$$

This rule, which has four terms and one applicability marker, (optional), is not only shorter than the ordered reduction rule, which has six terms and two markers (optional, mirror-image), but it would appear that its relative symbolic simplicity is directly associated with its superior expression of the fundamental features of the reduction process, a process which would probably be typically described in ordinary language simply as the elimination of the redundant elements of a coordination.

An effective utilization of either an ordered or an unordered reduction rule, such as (33) or (34), is possible only in grammars governed by certain crucial metatheoretical constraints on the analysis of variables. It should also be noted that both rules presuppose additional regrouping processes to account for facts about

---

subordinate syllabic or segmental constituents. (Compare the similar downward distribution of the negativity element, an axiomatic constituent of sentences, to certain subordinate segments of the sentence, e.g. determiners and modals. The negativity element can plausibly be posited as an axiomatic constituent of sentences, of course, only if it is an axiomatically UNORDERED constituent; the same is true for lexical features of backness, roundness, etc.) See Norman (1973) for more general and detailed discussion of the motivation for mirror-image conflations and the applicational relations of their subrules.

reductions with *respective(ly)*, etc., and that their structural descriptions may be inadequately specified even with respect to certain more ordinary types of reduction. However, all factors such as these are equally relevant to the two alternative formulations of reduction, and there is every reason to believe that the simplicity and naturalness of unordered reduction relative to ordered reduction would hold for all expansions of our domain of explanation. What is most important here, though, is the fact that unordered reduction is clearly POSSIBLE; thus even if it should ultimately turn out that an ordered reduction rule could be formulated which was simpler than an unordered one, it would still be the case that unordered reduction would have to be selected, since it is evidently only the latter which is compatible with any principled explanation of the directionality relation in reduced coordinations. Such an explanation would be possible for grammars containing ordered reduction rules only if ALL rules of grammars were mirror-image rules, in which case the directionality relation would follow necessarily from an independently-motivated metatheoretical principle. Thus unless the universality of mirror-image applicability could be demonstrated, — which is clearly impossible for ordered-base grammars — the derivational precedence of reduction to ordering must be considered necessary as well as sufficient.

It has been shown thus far that an adequate explanation of verbally-reduced coordinations in English- and Japanese-type languages can be effected by a theory which assumes that linguistic structures are axiomatically unordered in these languages and that coordination reduction applies to such unordered structures prior to the application of the general ordering rules which assign invariant orderings to the superficial subjects, verbs, and objects of all sentences. It remains now to determine whether this theory is also adequate with respect to the superficially more complex facts about verbally-reduced coordinations in Russian- and Hindi-type languages. Since evidence concerning these types forms the basis for Ross's argument for the necessity of re-ordering rules, successful extension of the unordered reduction theory to accomodate these data will constitute strong support for the assumption of invariant

derivational ordering. Since Ross's argument apparently constitutes one of the strongest and most explicit cases that has ever been made for axiomatic and variable ordering, and since the theory he formulates on the basis of these assumptions is demonstrably incapable of explaining the directionality relation in reduced coordinations of English- and Japanese-type languages, the explanatory deficiencies of this theory relative to the proposed unordered reduction alternative could also be EXPLAINED then as a consequence of the principle that there are NO explanatory grammatical theories which violate the Invariant Order Constraint.

The ordering of constituents in the reduced and unreduced clauses of English and Japanese, we may recall, is effected by the application of the general post-cyclic ordering rules

(35) (1a) [V, O] → [V & O]   (English)
      (1b) [V, O] → [O & V]   (Japanese)
      (2)   [S, O] → [S & O]   (English, Japanese).

Since Russian has both simple clauses and reduced coordinations of both the English-type (SVO; SVO and SO) and the Japanese-type (SOV; SO and SOV), it would be quite natural to assume that the ordering rules for Russian must involve a union of the English and Japanese rules. This is even more directly suggested by the fact that the generalization expressed by Rule (2), subjects precede objects, holds for all three language-types, while the union of (1a), verbs precede objects, and (1b), verbs follow objects, expresses a true generalization for Russian, namely that verbs either precede or follow their objects.

To adequately account for the facts about the ordering of clause constituents in Russian-type languages, then, one might simply assume that the grammars of these languages include the general ordering rule (2) and the union of Rules (1a) and (1b), which could be tentatively formulated as

(36) (1c) [X, Y] → [X & Y] (*where*: X = V or O; Y = V or O).

These rules would suffice for the derivation of the correct orderings of the constituents of unreduced clauses in Russian-type languages,

(37) $[S, [\underset{X}{V}, \underset{Y}{O}]]$ $[S, [\underset{Y}{V}, \underset{X}{O}]]$

| |

Rule 1c   Rule 1c

↓   ↓

$[S, [\underset{\overline{X}}{V} \& \underset{Y}{O}]]$ $[S, [\underset{X}{O} \& \underset{Y}{V}]]$

$\underset{\overline{S}}{\qquad} \underset{O}{\qquad}$ $\overline{S}\ \ O$

| |

Rule 2   Rule 2

↓   ↓

$[S \& [V \& O]]$ $[S \& [O \& V]]$

They would also suffice for the derivation of verbally-reduced alternants of both the English and Japanese type:

(38) $[S, [\underset{X}{V}, \underset{Y}{O}]], [S, O]$ $[S, [\underset{Y}{V}, \underset{X}{O}]], [S, O]$

$\overline{\qquad X \qquad}\ \ \overline{\quad Y \quad}$ $\overline{\quad Y \quad}\ \ \overline{\quad X \quad}$

| |

Rule 1c   Rule 1c

↓   ↓

$[S, [\underset{\overline{X}}{V} \& \underset{Y}{O}]] \& [S, O]$ $[S, O] \& [S, [\underset{X}{O} \& \underset{Y}{V}]]$

$\overline{\quad X \quad}\ \ \overline{\ Y\ }$ $\overline{\ X\ }\ \ \overline{\quad Y \quad}$

$\overline{S}\ \ \ O\ \ \ S\ \overline{O}$ $\overline{S}\ \overline{O}\ \ \ S\ \ O$

| |

Rule 2   Rule 2

↓   ↓

$[S \& [V \& O]] \& [S \& O]$ $[S \& O] \& [S \& [O \& V]]$

These rules do not suffice, however, for the derivation of the third type of Russian reduction, SOV and SO, a type which also occurs in Hindi but not in English or Japanese. They do not suffice, that is, as long as a uniformity constraint on the analysis of linguistic structures is maintained. This uniform analysis constraint, which has been tacitly assumed thus far with respect to ordering

rules as well as all other obligatory grammatical transformations, requires that if some constant of some string is analyzed as some variable of some rule that rule is applicable to the string only if all instances of the constant in the string are analyzed as that same variable and only if each of these constants undergoes each of the operations specified by the rule with respect to the given variable. In other words, this constraint, which appears to have been fairly widely accepted with respect to phonological rules, requires that structures be exhaustively and uniformly analyzed with respect to the structural descriptions of rules, and that once a particular analysis has been assigned, specified structural changes must be effected in a uniform and exhaustive manner only, that is, "across the board" with respect to all co-analyzed structures. Thus, to take the illustrated applications of Rule (1c) as an example, if ONE constituent including V is analyzed as X, then BOTH constituents including V (V and [S, [V, O]]) must be analyzed as X and BOTH will be ordered to the left of their sister Y constituents (O and [S, O]) by Rule (1c). Similarly, if O rather than V is analyzed as X, then both [O] and [S, O] will be so-analyzed and (1c) will effect the ordering of each of these to the left of their respective sisters, [V] and [S, [V, O]].

Since the uniform analysis constraint prevents the derivation of SOV and SO reductions in Russian by means of Rules (1c) and (2), we must either abandon these rules for Russian or else drop the uniform analysis constraint with respect to ordering rules. The latter alternative is clearly out of the question here, however, since the toleration of non-uniform analyses for Rule (1c) would expand its output in such a way as to include not only the desired [SOV and SO] structure but also the universally-ungrammatical structure [*SO and SVO]:

(39)   [S, [V, O]], [S, O]   [S, [V, O]], [S, O]

Rule 1c   Rule 1c

$$[S, [O \ \& \ V]] \ \& \ [S, O] \qquad\qquad [S, O] \ \& \ [S, [V \ \& \ O]]$$
$$\overline{X} \quad \overline{Y} \qquad\qquad\qquad\qquad\qquad \overline{X} \quad \overline{Y}$$

X	Y	X	Y
$\overline{S} \ O$	$\overline{S} \ O$	$\overline{S} \ O$	$\overline{S} \quad O$

Rule 2   Rule 2
↓   ↓

$[S \ \& \ [O \ \& \ V]]$ and $[S \ \& \ O]$ *$[S \ \& \ O]$ and $[S \ \& \ [V \ \& \ O]]$

Thus Rules (1c) and (2) are inadequate for Russian-type languages either with or without the uniform analysis constraint, in the former case because of failure to derive the grammatical reduction SOV and SO, in the latter case because of failure to exclude derivations of the ungrammatical reduction *SO and SVO. It is necessary to conclude, then, that Rules (1c) and (2) are not included in the grammars of these languages.

This conclusion is of considerable significance. First, because these rules must be incorrect NOT ONLY for Russian-type languages but for ANY type of natural language, since, according to Ross, there are NO known languages which have reduction sets equal to the output of (1c) and (2) either WITH uniform analysis, (38), or WITHOUT it, (38) and (39). Secondly, because this empirically-necessary exclusion of (1c) and (2) from all grammars actually follows from the fact that, in terms of any adequate theory of grammar, Rule (1c) is not a possible rule at all. It is not a possible rule because it is essentially associated with rule-specific conditions on analysis and applicability (X, Y = V, O), such conditions being properly excluded by explanatory theories of grammar. This metatheoretical exclusion is necessitated by the fact that no necessary explanatory purpose is served by any known conflation based upon rule-specific conditions, while the toleration of such conditions would allow for the formulation of conflated rules which are clearly grossly unnatural and which would typically obscure rather than reveal significant generalization about languages. The present facts show then that the exclusion of rule-specific conditions not only provides a desirable empirically-defensible narrowing

of the set of possible rules of grammar, but also that it serves the empirically-NECESSARY function of excluding Rule (1c) from the grammar of every natural language. Thus, since the exclusion of rule-specific conditions is obviously independent of any particular facts or rules about coordinative reduction, what we have here is an extremely general EXPLANATION of the fact that no natural language has verbally-reduced coordinations of the forms SVO and SO and SO and SOV and of no other form. In Ross's analysis this fact can be accounted for only by means of a number of highly specific assumptions about the existence and interrelationships of PARTICULAR rules and structures — e.g. the essentially *ad hoc* assumptions that gapping is directionally-restricted, that it both precedes and follows scrambling, that different languages have essentially different constituent-orderings before as well as after reduction, etc. Here, on the other hand, this fact is simply a necessary consequence of the assumption of a single independently-motivated metatheoretical constraint on the well-formedness of all grammatical rules, since the derivation of the universally non-occurring reduction set (SVO and SO, SO and SOV) requires the postulation of a rule (1c) which violates this universal constraint.

We thus have further evidence here of the superior explanatory value of the hypothesis of unordered reduction and of the metatheoretical assumption of invariant derivational ordering which motivates it. The present facts also lend considerable support to the independent metatheoretical principles of unconditionality and uniformity of analysis:

(40) (i) UNCONDITIONALITY. For any theory of grammar T and any statement R, R is a possible rule of some grammar governed by T only if every term and operation of R is UNCONDITIONALLY SELF-EXPLANATORY with respect to T, i.e. only if R is entirely free of non-universal conditions of analysis or applicability.

(ii) UNIFORM ANALYSIS. For any linguistic structure S and any grammatical rule R (where R is, in particular, an ordering rule, but, hypothetically, any obligatory

rule), *R* is applicable to *S* only if it is applied in such a way that for any two substructures *A* and *B* included in *S* and any variable *V* included in *R*, if *A* and *B* are co-generic (i.e. constituents of the same type) and co-analyzable as *V*, then if *A* is analyzed as *V*, *B* is also analyzed as *V*, and any operation effected with respect to *A* as an instance of *V* is also effected with respect to *B* as an instance of *V*.[16]

The substantiation of these principles and of the proposed hypotheses of unordered reduction and invariant ordering still depends, of course, on our ability to provide a substitute set of ordering rules for (1c) and (2) which will be compatible with the theory proposed thus far and which will allow for the principled derivation of precisely those three reduction-types which are grammatical in Russian. If this can be done, and if a compatible set of ordering rules can also be provided to account for the remaining set of Hindi-type data, the present case for the sufficiency and explanatory value of invariant ordering can be safely rested.

For Russian-type languages, then, although rules (1c) and (2) express true generalizations for Ross's chosen data domain, we can see that the following generalizations are also true with respect to all reduced and unreduced clauses in this domain:

[16]   Both of these principles are related to, but perhaps not fully subsumed by, the general metacondition that for any theory of grammar *T* and any rule *R* governed by *T*, the product of the application of *R* to any arbitrary representation *S* is fully determined by (*T*, *R*, *S*), where the product will be identical to *S* only if *R* is not applicable to it. This metacondition will be discussed subsequently in connection with Postal's (1971) Crossover Principle. If there are non-reapplicable rules defined on variables (e.g. feature exchange rules of the sort illustrated by Chomsky and Halle's [1968] formulation of the Great Vowel Shift in English), something like the Uniform Analysis Constraint is clearly needed. In its expository formulation here, however, the constraint is almost certainly inadequate as well as excessively cumbersome. It will also be observed that the Unconditionality Constraint is essentially identical to the hypothesis of Universally-Determined Rule-Application, which excludes all non-universal constraints on the directionality, obligatoriness, or applicational precedence relations of grammatical rules. See Sanders (1973) and the references cited there.

(41) (i) Either a subject constituent or a verb constituent
           precedes a sister object constituent;
      (ii) Either a subject constituent or an object constituent
           precedes a sister verb constituent.

This would suggest that the correct ordering rules for languages of
this type might be, rather than (1c) and (2), the rules

(42) (i) $[\begin{Bmatrix} S \\ V \end{Bmatrix}, O] \rightarrow [\begin{Bmatrix} S \\ V \end{Bmatrix} \& O]$

      (ii) $[\begin{Bmatrix} S \\ O \end{Bmatrix}, V] \rightarrow [\begin{Bmatrix} S \\ O \end{Bmatrix} \& V]$.

Since S and V constitute a natural class of non-objects, and since
S and O constitute a natural class of non-verbs, we can eliminate
the metatheoretically-unsatisfactory disjunctions of (42) and express
the content of these rules in the more normal form,

(43) (i) $[-O, O] \rightarrow [-O \& O]$ (A non-object precedes an
                                               object)
      (ii) $[-V, V] \rightarrow [-V \& V]$ (A non-verb precedes a verb),

where for any element, or structure, A, the notation $-A$ represents a
variable over the range of all element-sets or structures which do
not immediately include any instance of A.

We will now show that rules (i) and (ii) in their non-disjunctive
formulations (43) are entirely sufficient for the derivation of correct
superficial orderings of constituents in both simple clauses and
verbally-reduced coordinations of Russian-type languages. Thus,
for simple clauses, these rules, applied in either order, will effect
the following derivations:

(44)

$[S, [V, O]]$	$[S, [V, O]]$	$[S, [V, O]]$	$[S, [V, O]]$
$-O \quad O$	$\overline{V}\text{-}\overline{V}$	$-O \quad O$	$-V \quad V$
|	|	|	|
Rule i	Rule ii	Rule i	Rule ii
$\downarrow$	$\downarrow$	$\downarrow$	$\downarrow$

```
[S, [V & O]]        [S, [O & V]]        [S & [V, O]]        [S & [V, O]]
 -O̅   O̅              -V̅   V̅              -O̅    O̅             -V̅    V̅
[S, [V & O]]        [S, [O & V]]        [S & [V, O]]        [S & [V, O]]
 -V̅   V̅              -O̅   O̅              V̅ -V̅               -O̅    O̅
     |                   |                   |                   |
  Rule ii              Rule i              Rule ii             Rule i
     ↓                   ↓                   ↓                   ↓
[S & [V & O]]       [S & [O & V]]       [S & [O & V]]       [S & [V & O]]
```

The same rules, applying to alternate analyses of the unordered product of the universal coordinative reduction rule (34), will also effect the derivation of the three grammatical verbally-reduced coordinations of Russian-type languages, as shown in (45), page 55.

These derivations are entirely regular and in full conformity with the principle of uniform analysis. Since there are also correct derivations in which rule (ii) takes precedence over (i), and since these rules are not governed by any known universal constraint on applicational precedence, the proposed account is also fully consistent with the hypothesis of universally-determined rule-application (Sanders 1973). It should be noted, moreover, that in the derivation of [SVO and SO] reductions the sequential application of rules (i) and (ii) results in a structure which still includes an unordered substructure [S, O] which satisfies the structural description of rule (i). It is thus assumed here that rule (i) will properly apply again at this stage to effect a completion of the ordering derivation. Such non-consecutive cyclic reapplicability of rules is not necessary, however, since the [SVO and SO] reduction can also be derived simply by successive reapplications of rule (i), in accordance with the universal theory of rule-application presented in Ringen (1973). The correct orderings for Russian-type languages are thus derivable by highly-restrictive theories of grammar in an entirely regular and non *ad hoc* manner. The same is true for the final case of ordering in Hindi-type languages.

In these languages, we may recall, the order of constituents in simple clauses is SOV and all verbally-reduced coordinations are of the form [SO and SOV] or [SOV and SO]. Comparing these data

(45)

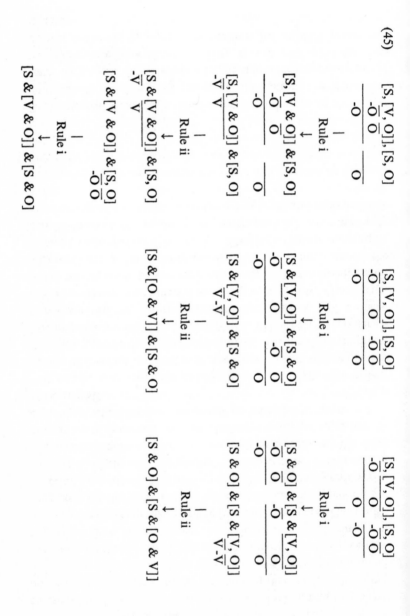

to those for Japanese-type languages, we note that the simple clauses of both language-types are identical (SOV), that they share one reduction-type (SO and SOV), and that they differ with respect to ordering only in that Hindi-type languages have one additional reduction (SOV and SO) which is ungrammatical in Japanese-type languages. This would suggest a basic similarity of some sort between the ordering rules of these two language-types. This is also suggested by the fact that the generalizations expressed by the ordering rules for the Japanese-type — (1b) 'objects precede verbs' and (2) 'subjects precede objects' — also can be interpreted as true generalizations about the Hindi-type structures. We have already seen, however, that the Japanese ordering rules are incapable of effecting the derivation of the Hindi-type reduction SOV and SO.

It can be seen from the Hindi-type data, though, that in languages of this type nominal constituents are always ordered before their non-superordinate sister constituents. Thus, subject nominals (the immediately included N's in [N, [N, V]] or [N [N]] constructions) are ordered before their unreduced ([N, V]) or reduced ([N]) predicates; and object nominals (the N's in [N, V] constructions) are ordered before their sister verbs. For mutually non-superordinate nominal constituents (like the conjuncts of the reduced coordination [[N, [N, V]], [N, [N]]]) either constituent can be ordered before the other, with each such ordering being an ordering of a nominal constituent before its non-superordinate sister.

This generalization about Hindi-type languages can be formally expressed by the ordering rule (46).

(46) $[N, [X]] \rightarrow [N \& [X]]$

This rule will clearly specify the correct orderings of the major constituents of all simple transitive and intransitive clauses in these languages. When applied to the universal representation of verbally-reduced coordinations (30), it will also yield the two correct orderings of such coordinations for all Hindi-type languages:

(47)

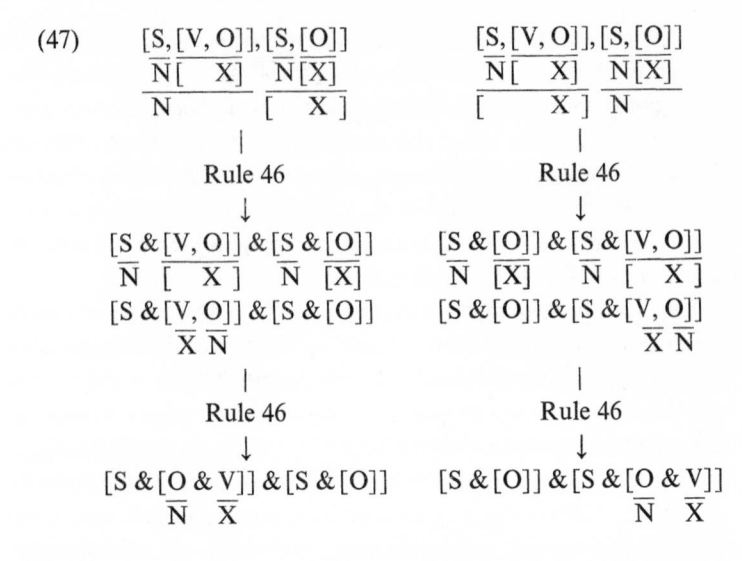

All of Ross's facts about verbally-reduced coordinations in natural language can thus be explained in a very simple and natural way by means of a theory that makes no use whatever of reordering rules and is thus fully consistent with the Invariant Order Constraint. This theory depends in an essential way on the metatheoretical assumption that all underlying structures are axiomatically unordered and that all ordering rules observe the general constraints of uniform analysis, unconditionality, and universally-determined rule-application. The assumption of order-free underlying structures is necessary because it makes available as an empirical hypothesis the explanatorily crucial assumption that coordination reduction is derivationally prior rather than subsequent to ordering in all phonetically-directed derivations. The observance by ordering rules of the unconditionality and uniform analysis constraints is necessary for the exclusion of the otherwise possible rule (1c), whose inclusion in any grammar would allow for the derivation of the universally ungrammatical reduction [*SO and SVO] or the universally non-occurring reduction set [SVO and SO, SO and SOV]. These assumptions are well-motivated independently of any facts about coordinative reduc-

tion, and each provides an explanatorily-valuable restriction of the class of possible grammars of natural languages. Their joint acceptance here thus allows for the principled explanation of a set of very specific facts about the ordering of constituents in verbally-reduced coordinations by means of a universal and unconditional unordered reduction rule and a small set of independently-motivated general ordering rules which apply to the constituents of unreduced and reduced clauses alike.

The greater generality and explanatory power of this theory relative to any theory which assumes the derivational precedence of ordering to reduction has been demonstrated. Thus in the version of ordered reduction proposed by Ross it is necessary to assume (1) a language-specific differentiation of the ordering of superficial subjects, objects, and verbs prior to the application of coordinative reduction, (2) a reduction rule which makes essential use of an *ad hoc* rule-specific directionality restriction or mirror-image applicability condition, (3) a non-universal "scrambling" rule for the optional postposing of verbs, (4) a specific rule-ordering restriction to the effect that coordinative reduction may either precede or follow verb postposing, (5) another *ad hoc* verb postposing rule, identical to the first and unique to Hindi-type languages, which applies obligatorily after the last possible application of reduction, and (6) a specific restriction to the effect that verbs can be postposed but not preposed in reduced coordinations. Individually, these assumptions involve the postulation of rules and constraints which lack independent empirical or metatheoretical justification. Jointly, they constitute a theory which is strikingly arbitrary, complex, and unnatural in comparison to the alternative theory of unordered reduction.

Moreover, as we have shown, there is no possible modification or refinement of the ordered reduction theory which will be capable of explaining the observed superficial directionality relation in reduced coordinations. Since this relation can be explained, along with all the other relevant facts, by means of a very natural un-ordered reduction theory whose principles are all quite general and fully motivated independently of any facts about coordination, it

is reasonable to seek some metatheoretical basis for the greater explanatory power of the unordered reduction theory and for the inherent inadequacies of the contradictory theory of ordered reduction.

The empirical hypothesis that ordering precedes coordinative reduction is equally compatible with the contradictory metatheoretical assumptions that underlying structures are ordered and that underlying structures are unordered. However, all ordered reduction theories such as Ross's depend essentially on one or more reordering rules and are thus incompatible with the metatheoretical requirement of invariant ordering. To exclude the explanatorily less valuable hypothesis of ordered reduction, therefore, while allowing and motivating the more valuable hypothesis of unordered reduction, it is both necessary and sufficient to accept the Invariant Order Constraint as a universal principle of grammar.

TEST II: THE COMPLEX NP CONSTRAINT

Linguists such as Postal (1971) and Ross (1967) have proposed a number of general metatheoretical constraints on the applicability of rules effecting the linear as well as structural movement, or reordering, of grammatical constituents. Like all other grammatical constraints, these are intended to perform the empirically necessary function of excluding various particular ungrammatical derivations by means of abstract general principles governing the possible analysis and transformation of all possible linguistic objects. If a theory of grammar allows for the possibility of reordering rules, these rules will, of course, be governed by all the universal constraints of the theory, but it might also be the case that one or more of these constraints might conceivably be formulated in such a way that a violation of the constraint would be logically possible ONLY with respect to the application of rules which effect a reordering of constituents. Constraints of the latter sort could be said to depend ESSENTIALLY on the existence of reordering rules, and they obviously could not possibly be imposed by any metatheory which also imposes the Invariant Order Constraint. Thus if it could be shown that there are some linguistic facts which can be reasonably accounted for ONLY as a consequence of such an ESSENTIALLY movement-dependent constraint, it would necessarily follow that reordering rules are necessary and thus that the invariant order constraint is incorrect.

No evidence of this sort has been presented with respect to any of the movement constraints proposed thus far by Postal and Ross or others. The discriminatory effect of each of these constraints

can, in fact, quite readily be achieved, it appears, by means of
more general constraints on the scope of analysis or regrouping
functions of all grammatical rules, constraints which are independent of the existence or non-existence of reordering rules and which
in the latter case would be necessarily and sufficiently applicable
with respect to independently-motivated ordering or grouping
transformations.[1] This appears to be the case even for the superficially quite strongly order-dependent crossover constraint proposed by Postal (1971). There are, in fact, some reasons for believing that evidence of the necessity of movement constraints will
never be found in the domain of natural languages, and that any
purportedly-useful constraint of this sort will always be reducible
in a principled way to a constraint of equal or greater generality
which is applicable to grammars which uniformly observe the
invariant ordering constraint as well. We will now consider a few
of the reasons for this belief.

It is important to note first, though, that, since linear-movement-
dependent constraints are logically possible for any metatheory
which does not include an invariant ordering constraint, and since
Ross and Postal both assume a metatheory of that sort, it is entirely
reasonable and appropriate for them to have formulated their
rule-constraints in such a way that they are partly or wholly
effective with respect to reordering rules. Similarly, since their
metatheory allows for the possibility of reordering rules, it is quite
natural that they have chosen to illustrate their constraints with
respect to particular reordering rules which have been proposed in
grammars governed by that same metatheory. But the fact that
movement-constraints CAN be effectively used in variable-order
theories obviously does not prove that they MUST be used. On the
contrary, in fact, there is some evidence to suggest that EVEN for
metatheories which ALLOW reordering, all effects of any useful

---

[1] This appears to be implicit in many of the results of the research of Ross
(1967) and Postal (1971) themselves, since most of their major explanatory
concepts — e.g. the notions of syntactic islands, bounding, peerhood, pied-
piping — involve CONSTITUENCY relations, the relative ORDER of constituents
being entirely IRRELEVANT to the definition or explanatory function of the concept in question.

movement-constraint can be at least equally appropriately achieved by the application of movement-independent analysis, derivation, and scope constraints to non-movement rules which are motivated independently of the existence or non-existence of reordering rules. This is strongly suggested by the fact that every general constraint which has thus far been proposed as a movement constraint makes essential reference to constituency, or grouping, relations such as "dominates", "commands", "includes", etc., which are independent of the nature or existence of any ordering of the constituents so-related. Since all non-movement rule-constraints also make essential use of exactly these same order-independent relations, it is natural to conclude that what is actually constrained by all universal rule-constraints is the possible variability of grouping or association relations in the representations of the same linguistic object. All purported constraints on linear movement would thus really be constraints on non-linear regrouping which accidentally happen to be violable with respect to the analysis or operation of some set of postulated reordering rules. If this is true then it would still be possible to demonstrate the incorrectness of the invariant order constraint, but only if it could be shown that for at least one language there is some grouping constraint which is empirically necessary for the exclusion of some set of ungrammatical structures, but where the ONLY motivated rules which are both applicable to such structures and relevant to the given constraint are reordering rules.

To demonstrate the necessity of reordering for constraint violability, in other words, it would be necessary to find a violable movement rule whose structural description and output description are necessarily distinct from any possible analysis of the descriptions of every non-movement rule of the grammar. But we know that in natural languages differences in order are apparently invariably associated with other co-variant differences in structure — e.g. differences in (superficial) case and mood, and in the prosodically-significant grouping of constituents. Thus, for example, the order alternation between active and passive sentences in English is associated with co-variant alternations in the super-

ficial case properties of the alternately ordered nominals, in the mood of their intervening verb, and in the grouping of the verb relative to each of the nominals. (The necessity for regrouping is shown by the identical behavior of active and passive subjects and of active and passive predicates with respect to the general process of coordinative reduction.) The domains for the specification of each of these alternations are essentially identical, namely some structure of the form $[N_1 [V N_2]]$. Now if it were the case that an effective characterization of the ordering alternation here required the addition of variables in the structural description of a traditional passivization reordering rule so that the domain of this rule was of the form, say $[N_1 [X V N_2 Y]]$, it is clear that this same expansion would also be required then for the rules which add or change the mood features of the verb and the case features of the nominals. Thus any analysis constraint which might be violated with respect to the structural description of the passive reordering rule by some structure S would also be necessarily violated by S with respect to the structural descriptions of the passive verb-mood and nominal-case rules. Thus if we were to retain these non-movement passive rules but eliminate the passive reordering rule (e.g. in favor of general superficial ordering rules of the sort previously discussed), this elimination would have no effect whatever on the effective characterization of S with respect to its possible violation of any possible analysis constraint that is relevant to the structural description $[N_1 [X V N_2 Y]]$.

Such evidence of the non-necessity of a movement rule with respect to the discriminatory functions of some particular set of universal constraints will be available whenever the essential domain of the movement rule is also the domain of some non-movement rule. Althought it obviously cannot be DEMONSTRATED that this will always be the case for all possible languages, a strong reason for ASSUMING that it will always be the case is provided by the fact that the order alternations which have thus far been observed and described all appear to be associated with co-variant alternations in grouping and other properties of constituency and composition. Furthermore, of the actual reordering transforma-

tions which have thus far been proposed for various languages, all require the joint or subsequent application of the elementary operation of grouping, and most are also associated, like the traditional English passive transformation, with various processes of adjunction, deletion, and feature-specification as well. Finally, since any reordering rule is analyzable as a conflation of instances of the mutually-independent elementary transformations of (1) iteration, or identity adjunction, (2) identity deletion, (3) grouping, or association, and (4) ordering, a constraint which is uniquely applicable to reordering rules would, in a strict sense, be logically impossible except as an extra-systemic conceptualization of the intersection of the constraint-sets of precisely these four elementary operations. Whatever might appear to be a constraint on movement must thus really be a set of one or more constraints on one or more of the elementary transformations which constitute every movement rule. Thus since any reordering conflation can evidently be replaced without loss of explanatory power by an (intrinsically) ordered set of its included elementary transformations, it can only be concluded that the notion of constraints on reordering, like the notion of reordering itself, has no empirical significance with respect to natural languages and no systematic value in any explanatory theory about such languages.

All of the preceding considerations strongly suggest the hypothesis that all motivated grammatical constraints are compatible with the invariant order constraint, and that reordering is thus metatheoretically as well as empirically unnecessary. Suggestion is not demonstration, however, and in order to fully substantiate this hypothesis it would obviously be desirable to show, for each of the linear movement constraints that has been proposed thus far by Ross and others, that the explanatory functions of that constraint can be fully achieved without loss of generality by alternate rules and constraints which are wholly consistent with the principle of invariant ordering. Such an endeavor would obviously be far beyond the scope of the present study, however, since it would not only require the detailed critical analysis of each proposed constraint, with special reference to its explanatory range and depen-

dency relations with each other constraint. It would also require a similar analysis of each of the particular reordering rules which have been assumed as bases for the constraint's applicability. It is possible, nevertheless, to indicate the general lines that such demonstrations will take.

For this purpose we will briefly consider two typical movement constraints and the manner in which their explanatory functions can be achieved when movement-rules are metatheoretically excluded. We will first take up in this chapter a typical constraint of Ross's (1967), the Complex NP Constraint, with respect to the typical explanatory function of characterizing well-formed relative and interrogative structures. In the following chapter, we will then consider a somewhat different type of movement constraint, the derivational crossover restriction proposed by Postal (1971), with respect to the explanation of certain interesting restrictions on the ordering and functional relations of coreferential agents, patients, and oblique nominals in English. These examples appear to be fairly representative of the range of possible types of linear movement-constraints, and they illustrate their applicability with respect to both obligatory and optional transformations which are quite typical of those found in conventional variable-order grammars. The evidence of their non-necessity to be presented here can thus presumably be used, with appropriate modifications in details, to show the non-necessity of many other particular movement constraints which have been or might be proposed.

Ross's Complex NP Constraint requires that, for any NP_1 immediately dominating NP_2 and S, and for any constituent C included in S, no grammatical rule can effect a reordering of constituents such that C is not included in NP_1. Or, in Ross's words, "No element contained in a sentence dominated by a noun phrase with a lexical head noun may be moved out of that noun phrase by a transformation" (Ross 1967: 4.20, p. 127).[2]

[2] Ross restricts the domain of his constraint to noun phrases with "lexical head nouns" in order to, in his words, "distinguish between lexical items like *claim* in (4.17a) or *girl* in (4.14) on the one hand, and the abstract pronoun *it*

The Complex NP Constraint can actually be interpreted much more naturally as a derivational constraint than as a constraint on analysis, but in either case it is impossible to avoid the obvious conclusion that what is really involved here is a constraint on the possible grouping and associativity of constituents and not on their relative order or possible change of order.

Interpreted as a derivational movement constraint, Ross's version of the Complex NP Constraint could be formulated as in (48).

(48) For any linguistic object L, D is a possible derivation of L only if, for any derivational line n included in D, if n is analyzable as EITHER

(a) ... $_{NP}[NP \& _S[X \& C \& Y]]$ ..., OR
(b) the mirror-image of (a),

then there is no derivational line m included in D, where m is subsequent to n and is analyzable as EITHER

(c) ... $_{NP}[NP \& _S[X \& Y]]$ ... C ..., OR
(d) the mirror-image of (c), OR
(e) ... C ... $_{NP}[NP \& _S[X \& Y]]$ ..., OR
(f) the mirror-image of (e),

where the constituents NP, X, C, Y of line m are derived respectively from the NP, X, C, Y of line n.

The quite unrevealing awkwardness of this formulation is clearly

---

of (4.13a) on the other. Since it is possible to move elements out of sentences in construction with the third of these, as (4.13a) attests, but not out of sentences in construction with the first two ((4.18a) and (4.15) are ungrammatical, it will be necessary for the theory of grammar to keep them distinct somehow" (Ross 1967: 128). The sentences referred to here are

(4.13a) This is a hat which I'm going to see to it that my wife buys
(4.18a) *The hat which I believed the claim that Otto was wearing is red
(4.15) *Who does Phineas know a girl who is jealous of?

The details of Ross's analysis of sentences such as (4.13a) are irrelevant to the present discussion, and all complex NP's will here be assumed to have ordinary non-pronominal heads.

All page references to Ross (1967) refer to the mimeographed edition distributed by the Indiana University Linguistics Club.

due in part to the empirically unmotivated assumption that the relevant constraint here is directionally-restricted, or non-symmetrical, i.e. that it must exclude only extraposition FROM the S of a complex NP and not also interposition INTO the S of such an NP. This assumption is certainly incorrect, however, since there are undoubtedly no motivated rules about natural languages which require EITHER interposition OR extraposition with respect to structures of this sort.[3]

Such bi-directional applicability is also intrinsic to the functions of analysis constraints such as the traditional A-over-A principle (see Chomsky [1964a], Ross [1967b: Ch. 2]), strictly derivational constraints such as Postal's (1971) crossover principle, as well as other proposed movement-rule constraints of Ross's, such as the Sentential Subject Constraint (Ross 1967: 241-255), and the Coordinate Structure Constraint (Ross 1967: 158-195). There is some reason, in fact, to believe that all motivated universal constraints on derivations will be found to be symmetrical in this sense, i.e. that all such constraints restrict simply the possible CO-OCCURRENCE of certain related lines in the derivation of any single linguistic object. We may thus tentatively assume the following meta-constraint on the possible derivational constraints which may be imposed by any theory of grammar:

---

[3] There are undoubtedly facts which would show that the prohibition of Complex NP Interposition is necessary as well as sufficient. The best example that I have been able to think of thus far, however, requires acceptance of the highly dubious assumption that subject-raising in English depends on the presence of *it* as the superordinate subject, and that, at the point when subject-raising applies, expletive *it* and anaphoric *it* are non-distinct. If these assumptions are accepted, along with the reasonably conventional assumption that subject-raising effects the replacement of a superordinate (*it*) subject with the (derived) subject of its sentential object, then the constraint against complex NP interposition is necessary to prevent the improper application of subject-raising in (ii), where the subject would have to be interposed into a relative clause, while allowing its application in (i):

(i) (a) [*It was believed* [*John* had gone]] — Subj. Raising →
  (b) [John was believed [had gone → to have gone]]

(ii) (a) [I told [the man [of whom *it was believed*]] [*John* had gone]]
  (b) *I told the man of whom John was believed to have gone

(49) For any universal theory of grammar T, C is a possible
      derivational constraint of T only if, for any linguistic
      representations A and B, if the derivation of A from B is
      prohibited by C, then the derivation of B from A is also
      prohibited by C.

This constraint, which follows from the general hypothesis of Equational Grammar (Sanders 1972), is of considerable independent
interest as an explanans for a wide range of observed limitations on
the variability of natural languages. For present purposes, however,
it will suffice to consider it as merely providing an explanation for
the empirical non-significance of the relative derivational order of
the interpositive (n) and extrapositive (m) representations of (48).

Even when we eliminate the directionality restriction, however,
the fundamental inadequacy of the formulation (48) still remains:
namely, the logically-redundant and empirically-non-significant
specification that NEITHER of TWO (mirror-imaging) interpositional
structures may be co-derivational with ANY of FOUR (pairwise
mirror-imaging) extrapositional structures. This order-dependent
redundancy is clearly scientifically intolerable, and not merely
"inelegant", since it effectively PRECLUDES any expression of a
significantly more general grammatical principle: namely, that the
structure of any sentence in a complex NP is NON-ASSOCIATIVE
with respect to ANY structure not included in that NP, i.e. that
there can be no regrouping such that any constituent included in
S and any constituent not included in its NP are grouped as sister
constituents.

This fundamental inadequacy of the derivational formulation
(48) of the Complex NP Constraint is clearly a direct consequence
of the assumption that this constraint applies with respect to
structures which are wholly or partially ORDERED. But this assumption would obviously be a NECESSARY one if EVERY line of a derivation were ordered, this being the case if and only if it is assumed
that underlying structures are ordered. It follows, therefore, that
any theory of grammar that accepts axiomatic ordering will
necessarily fail to capture the generalization that the constituents

of a nominally-attributive clause are associative only within their including nominal phrase. Since this appears to constitute a particularly striking falsification of the ordered base hypothesis, it is worth restating the argument here in slightly more detail.

Let us assume, then, for the sake of the argument, that there is some grammar of a natural language which generates or accepts ordered underlying structures as the initiations of phonetically-terminated derivations. Every line of every derivation justified by this grammar will thus consist of a representation in which some elements are ordered either to the left or to the right of some other elements. (It is also assumed, of course, that there are no rules which could eliminate and then subsequently reintroduce all ordering relations in the middle of a derivation; even if such an arbitrary evasion were allowed, though, it would have no effect on the present argument unless the fancied medial suppression of ordering were co-terminous with the applicability of all transformations having any effect on constituency relations.)

To correctly apply to the derivations of this grammar, then, the Complex NP Constraint must be formulated in such a way as to explicitly prohibit the derivational co-occurrence of ANY one of TWO distinctively different interpositional representations (50) with ANY one of FOUR distinctively different extrapositional representations (51-52):

(50) a. $_{NP}[NP \&\ _{S}[X \& C \& Y]]$
      b. $_{NP}[\ _{S}[Y \& C \& X] \& NP]$

(51) a. $_{NP}[NP \&\ _{S}[X \& Y]] \ldots C \ldots$
      b. $\ldots C \ldots\ _{NP}[NP \&\ _{S}[X \& Y]]$

(52) a. $_{NP}[\ _{S}[Y \& X] \& NP] \ldots C \ldots$
      b. $\ldots C \ldots_{NP}[\ _{S}[Y \& X] \& NP]$

Applied to this axiomatically-ordered grammar the constraint must thus exclude eight distinct pairs of representations from any of its derivations. The specification of this exclusion can be reduced from a sixteen-string list of pairs to a six-string pair of disjunctions by use of an *ad hoc* and properly prohibited extension of the ordi-

nary abbreviatory conventions for disjunctive representations of linguistic structures:[4]

[4] The illegitimate extension here violates the first principle of significant conflation, namely, that representations can be conflated only if they are PARTLY IDENTICAL. To tolerate the specification of relations between ANY pair of disjunctive sets would be to falsely claim empirical significance for any number of absurd statements such as

(i) $\begin{Bmatrix} [CANINE] \\ [FELINE] \end{Bmatrix} = \begin{Bmatrix} animal \\ pet \end{Bmatrix}$

(ii) $\begin{Bmatrix} AGT \& V \& ACC \& DAT \\ ACC \& V \& DAT \& AGT \end{Bmatrix} \rightarrow \begin{Bmatrix} DAT \& V \& ACC \& AGT \\ AGT \& V \& DAT \& ACC \end{Bmatrix}$

The intended interpretation of (53) also requires that there be no relation between the order of members of one disjunction and the order of members of the other; this would be possible only if the order of members in both disjunctions is non-sequential, thereby violating the second most important principle of significant conflation: that conflatable statements always have an empirically significant sequential order relation to each other. (The converse of this may also be true too, i.e. that the only statements which are applicationally ordered with respect to each other are statements which are substantively related, that is, partially identical and conflatable.) In fact Chomsky (1967) has proposed that the subrules of disjunctive conflations are INVARIABLY applied CONJUNCTIVELY — i.e. SEQUENTIALLY. With respect to disjunctive conflation in particular, moreover, it appears that significance can be assured for such conflations only if they are required to be reducible to the standard form

$$A \rightarrow \begin{Bmatrix} B/C\underline{\qquad}D \\ ... \\ K \end{Bmatrix}$$

where the order of lines in the disjunction formally expresses the relative markedness and regularity relations among all the substatements of the conflation, the first being the most marked and most exceptional member of the set, the last context-free member being the most unmarked and widely-distributed member, the "basic" or "major" statement in the set. This last restriction might initially seem too strong, however, since context-free disjunctive statements have been used sometimes as a means for the expression of significant precedence relations. Thus the hierarchical precedence relation governing the process of vowel reduction in Modern Greek could be expressed by Bach's context-free sequentially-ordered disjunctive statement (1968: 133):

$$V \rightarrow \emptyset / \begin{Bmatrix} a \\ o \\ u \\ i \end{Bmatrix} +$$

Similar use could be made of such context-free disjunctions for the specification of the precedence relation between Agents and Instruments with respect to the process of subject-formation in English,

(53)
$$\begin{Bmatrix} (50a) \\ (50b) \end{Bmatrix} \neq \begin{Bmatrix} (51a) \\ (51b) \\ (52a) \\ (52b) \end{Bmatrix}$$

Since the strings of the left disjunction here, (50a) and (50b), stand in a mirror-image relation to each other, the acceptance of a general convention for mirror-image conflation would allow us to eliminate this disjunction in favor of a single generalized string representation, which we may call for convenience of reference (M.I. 50 ab). Turning now to the right disjunction of (53), we find that representations (51a) and (52b) are mirror-images of each other, as are (51b) and (52a). Given the power of mirror-image conflation, then, this disjunction can be reduced from four terms to two, (M.I. 51a-52b) and (M.I. 51b-52a). No further conflation is possible, however, in terms of any known or presently conceivable principles for the empirically-significant abbreviation of linguistic representations. Thus, if the Complex NP Constraint needs to be applicable to ordered structures, its optimally general formulation will be

(54) COMPLEX NP CONSTRAINT ON ORDERED STRUCTURES
(Mirror-Image)
$$_{NP}[NP \ \& \ _S[X \ \& \ C \ \& \ Y]] \neq \begin{Bmatrix} _{NP}[NP \ \& \ _S[X \ \& \ Y]] \ldots C \ldots \\ \ldots C \ldots \ _{NP}[NP \ \& \ _S[X \ \& \ Y]] \end{Bmatrix}$$

$$[\begin{Bmatrix} [AGENT] \\ [INSTR] \end{Bmatrix}, [VERB], X] \rightarrow [\begin{Bmatrix} [AGENT] \\ [INSTR] \end{Bmatrix} [[VERB], X]]$$

as well as many other parallel hierarchical restrictions on grouping and ordering. The problem with all statements of this sort, though, is that while they explicitly reveal the precedence relations that actually hold in the derivation of well-formed linguistic objects, they obviously preclude any explanation of why certain structures take precedence over certain others. See Sanders (1970) for a general discussion of precedence relations and proposed explanations of the particular precedences for Greek elision and English subjecthood. See also Chapter 4.

It should be noted that the non-equivalence connective in (53) simply stands for the relation of derivational non-cooccurrence, or mutual non-derivability. Thus it follows from $A \neq B$ that there is no well-formed derivation with lines analyzable both as XAY and as XBY. See Sanders (1972) for evidence of the appropriateness of non-equivalence statements for the expression of all significant global or prohibitive rules of grammar.

It should be noted that, while the members of the remaining extra-positional disjunction still reveal obvious mirror-image-like relations, these representations cannot be further reduced without loss of essential information. What prevents further generalization is actually the fact that the order of the extraposed constituent and its NP, the order of the head and attributive S of the NP, and the order of the variables X and Y within the attributive S are all entirely INDEPENDENT of each other. The mutual independence of the orderings of these constituents, and the fact that the Complex NP Constraint must apply to all permutations of their permutations, indicates once again that order is IRRELEVANT to the function of this constraint and thus that the constraint can be appropriately specified only with respect to UNORDERED structures. This conclusion is reflected and formally demonstrated by the fact that even with the powerful aid of mirror-image conflation, and even if we allow the abbreviatory use of randomly ordered context-free disjunctions, such usage being properly excluded for all other representations of linguistic structures, it is still impossible to reduce this constraint to a simple statement of the derivational non-co-occurrence of TWO generalized structures. But such reduction is necessary for the explanatory purpose of revealing precisely those identities and differences which are necessary and sufficient for the prediction of the relevant non-co-occurrence in any possible derivation. Since the requisite reduction is impossible, given the assumption that there is some grammar that accepts ordered representations as initiations of its derivations, and since, given the contradiction of this assumption, it IS possible to achieve the reduction, we can only conclude that the assumption that axiomatic ordering is possible is false and that its contradiction, i.e. the Unordered Base Constraint, is a true assumption about the nature of natural language.

For all grammatical theories which observe the Unordered Base Constraint, the Complex NP Constraint can be expressed by means of the following simple statement of the derivational mutual exclusivity of two related structures:

(55) COMPLEX NP CONSTRAINT ON UNORDERED STRUCTURES
$_{NP}[NP, _s[C, X]] \neq _{NP}[NP, _s[X]], \ldots C \ldots$

Since the elementary transformation of ordering applies, by metatheoretical definition, only to constituents of the same construction, all rules effecting changes in grouping, or constituency, relations must necessarily apply prior to the application of ordering. Thus the Complex NP Constraint is logically and empirically relevant only to those lines of any axiomatically unordered derivation which are derived prior to the application of ordering rules, since it is precisely with respect to those lines that grouping is variable. And it is precisely with respect to these order-free lines that (55) is effectively applicable. The Unordered Base Constraint is thus fully compatible with the Complex NP Constraint and clearly necessary for its optimally general expression as a constraint on derivational co-occurrence.

Exactly the same arguments apply if the Complex NP Constraint is interpreted as a constraint on analysis rather than derivation. Thus for all theories of grammar which do not incorporate the Unordered Base Constraint it is necessary to exclude any rule whose structural description (input analysis) or product description (output analysis) can be analyzed in such a way as to include both a structure that is within the S of a complex NP and a structure that is outside that NP, for all possible permutations, again, of all the relevant constituents. Allowing for mirror-image conflation, the optimal generality that can be achieved for such theories is a list of TWO prohibited rule-analyses, each a mirror-image conflation, and not further reducible without loss of essential information:

(56) *Rule: M.I. ... $_{NP}[NP \& _s[X \& C \& Y]] \ldots D \ldots$
     *Rule: M.I. ... D ... $_{NP}[NP \& _s[X \& C \& Y]] \ldots$

For theories which include the Unordered Base Constraint, on the other hand, a necessary and sufficient formulation of the Complex NP restriction as an analysis constraint will consist of a list of only ONE prohibited rule-analysis:

(57)   COMPLEX NP CONSTRAINT ON UNORDERED STRUCTURES
       (Analysis)
       *Rule: ... ₙₚ[NP, ₛ[C, X]], ... D ...

Thus, whether formulated as a constraint on derivations or on
rule-analyses, the Complex NP Constraint is most appropriately
specified with respect to unordered structures, an optimally general
and revealing formulation of the constraint hence being possible
only for theories of grammar which also include the Unordered
Base Constraint. Moreover, since this constraint deals essentially
with the grouping of constituents irrespective of their ultimate
order, it is clearly compatible with any system of either variable or
invariant derivational ordering, as long as constituency relations
remain invariant under all ordering and reordering transformations.
In other words, the Complex NP Constraint depends essentially
on the Unordered Base Constraint and is compatible with the
Invariant Order Constraint; it would be compatible with the
existence of re-ordering rules only if these, like ordering rules, were
restricted in their possible effect to the specification of ordering
relations between sister constituents of the same construction.
    There is apparently no other way to interpret the Complex NP
Constraint without completely destroying its explanatory filtering
function. Thus, although Ross consistently refers to this constraint
as a "constraint on reordering transformations", and gives, as its
most explicit formulation, the statement that "No element contained in a sentence dominated by a noun phrase with a lexical
head noun may be moved out of that noun phrase by a transformation" (Ross 1967: 127), it can readily be seen that to achieve the
avowed purposes of the constraint it is neither necessary nor
sufficient that reorderings be constrained, and though it would
suffice to constrain the OPERATIONS of ALL rules, it is NOT NECESSARY
to constrain ANY operation. For if the Complex NP Constraint
were really applicable ONLY to RULES which effect a REORDERING
of constituents, the constraint clearly would have no explanatory
filtering effect whatever, since any derivation which is supposed to
be excluded by the constraint can be effected by the application of a

sequence of reordering rules, none of which violates the constraint, or by a sequence of iteration and deletion rules, none of which effects any reordering of constituents at all.

Thus, for example, although Ross explicitly wishes the Complex NP Constraint to exclude derivations such as (58a), if we were to take his rule-operational formulation of the constraint literally, we would have no way of excluding the sequential versions of this derivation, (58b) and (58c), which, though clearly violating the SPIRIT of the constraint, certainly do not violate its operational LETTER:

(58)

(a) $_{NP}[NP_1 \; _{NP}[NP_2 \; _S[X \; NP_3 \; Y]]] \rightarrow *_{NP}[NP_1 \; NP_3 \; _{NP}[NP_2 \; _S[X \; Y]]]$

(b) $[NP_1 \; [NP_2 \; [X \; NP_3 \; Y]]]$—Rule n (reordering) →
$[NP_1 \; [NP_2 \; NP_3 \; [X \; Y]]]$—Rule n + m (reordering) →
$[NP_1 \; NP_3 \; [NP_2 \; [X \; Y]]]$

(c) $[NP_1 \; [NP_2 \; [X \; NP_3 \; Y]]]$—Rule n (iteration, grouping, ordering) →
$[NP_1 \; NP_3 \; [NP_2 \; [X \; NP_3 \; Y]]]$—Rule n + m (deletion) →
$[NP_1 \; NP_3 \; [NP_2 \; [X \; Y]]]$

Since reordering is not an elementary operation of any known explanatory theory of grammar, it will always be possible in axiomatically-ordered grammars to achieve the effect of any reordering by an indefinitely large and indefinitely unrelated set of non-reordering rules. Any purported operational constraint on reordering will thus necessarily fail to achieve its intended explanatory purpose, since any derivation that is DIRECTLY prohibited by the constraint can be effected INDIRECTLY WITHOUT violation of that constraint. This simply shows once again that the notion "constraint on reordering" is devoid of empirical significance in linguistics. But if there are no empirical constraints on reordering, then it must also be the case that the notion of reordering itself is devoid of linguistic significance.

We have shown thus far, with respect to the Complex NP Constraint, a purported constraint on reordering, that the constraint cannot be interpreted as a constraint on the operation of reordering

rules, and that when it is interpreted in functionally adequate ways, as a constraint either on derivational co-occurrence or on possible rule-analyses, the constraint is most simply and most revealingly formulated with respect to the grouping relations of unordered constituents. The explanatory functions of this constraint can be adequately achieved then only with respect to unordered structures and the transformational rules which apply to such structures, that is, only with respect to grammars which accept axiomatically unordered structures and which specify superficial ordering relations by post-cyclic ordering rules which are defined solely on superficial groupings. The most natural and most general formulation of the Complex NP Constraint thus depends essentially on the acceptance of the Unordered Base Constraint and is wholly compatible with the Invariant Order Constraint.

All of the preceding arguments appear to be generally applicable to all purported constraints on reordering which have been proposed thus far. Thus, regardless of the ultimate correctness or independence of the Complex NP Constraint, the Crossover Principle, the Sentential Subject Constraint, etc., it appears to be necessarily the case, if our arguments have at all been valid, that NO grammatical constraint can ever depend ESSENTIALLY on the existence or possibility of derivational changes in ordering.

The fact that no constraint depends ESSENTIALLY on reordering obviously does not necessarily imply, however, that it could never be the case that the proper function of some constraint might depend ACCIDENTALLY in some language on the possibility of reordering in that language. That is, it is conceivable that in some language there might be certain incorrect derivations which can be excluded only by means of a certain well-motivated universal constraint, where the conditions for the possible violation of that constraint can be effected in that language in a motivated way ONLY if it is possible for constituents to be derivationally reordered in that language. The Invariant Order Constraint implies that this situation, though logically possible, will never actually arise with respect to the domain of all possible natural languages. Although it is obviously impossible to demonstrate the truth of this claim

without having access to a "perfect" grammar of every possible language, there appears to be no reason to doubt its truth thus far. Moreover, since the Invariant Order Constraint determines a narrower characterization of natural language than its contradiction, the burden of proof is properly on the proponents of those theories that violate Invariant Ordering. Nevertheless, to conclude this discussion on a less abstract note, we will now attempt to show how some of the intended explanatory functions of the Complex NP Constraint can be achieved by theories of grammar which observe the Invariant Order Constraint.

Among the facts which the Complex NP Constraint is intended to account for is the fact that, in English and, presumably, all other languages, a relative or interrogative clause is well-formed only if the relative or interrogative constituent is not derived from any constituent which is included in a relative clause subordinate to the clause to which its head is (directly) attributed (cf. Ross [1967: 118-158], Chomsky [1964b]). Thus, it is necessary to allow for the derivation of sentences such as (59b) in which the relative derives from a non-subordinate constituent of an attributive clause, while excluding all sentences such as (60b) in which the relative could only be derived from a constituent which is included in a relative clause which is itself included in the attributive clause.

(59) (a) *The dog* [the boy was chasing *that dog*] was barking
     (b) The dog that the boy was chasing was barking
(60) (a) *The dog* [the boy [that boy was chasing *that dog*] was laughing] was barking
     (b) *The dog that the boy that was chasing (it) was laughing was barking

Exactly the same restriction holds with respect to the relatives in complete and truncated interrogative sentences, such as

(61) (a) Tell me (the identity of) *that thing* [the boy was chasing *that thing*]
     (b) Tell me (the identity of) that thing that the boy was chasing

    (c) Tell me what the boy was chasing
    (d) What was the boy chasing
(62) (a) Tell me (the identity of) *that thing* [the boy [that boy
          was chasing *that thing*] was laughing]
    (b) *Tell me (the identity of) that thing that the boy that
          was chasing (it) was laughing
    (c) *Tell me what the boy that was chasing (it) was
          laughing
    (d) *What was the boy that (was) chasing (it) was laughing

Numerous other semantic and formal relations between questions
and relatives have been observed, of course, in English and a wide
variety of other languages.[5] For information, or WH-type, questions at least, the superficially "simple" and "interrogative" alternants can be derived in a quite natural and straightforward way
by optional reductions of the structures underlying their relativized
imperative paraphrases (cf. Sanders 1967, Koutsoudas 1968). Since
this is the only presently-known way of achieving a principled
explanation of the various known relations between questions,
imperatives, and relatives in natural languages, and since it appears
to be also compatible with various motivated treatments of truth-
value, or yes-no, questions, and other related constructions, we
will tentatively assume that all of the following hypotheses are true:

    (i) The universal set of elements, in terms of which all possible
linguistic representations and rules are formulated, contains no
element (such as the traditional Q or WH) which is semantically
interpreted as "questioned proposition", "I request that you tell
me ..." (cf. Katz and Postal 1964), or the like; in other words, all
underlying structures are free of interrogative elements or operators.[6]

---

[5] Thus, for example, in Temne (Sierra Leone), as reported by Larry Hutchin-
son (personal communication), the tenses of interrogative sentences are restricted to a proper subset of the tenses occurring in simple declaratives, and
the tenses of relative clauses are restricted to exactly the same subset. Similar
syntactic relations between relative and interrogative clauses have been reported
for Ojibwe by Tim Dunnigan and Ken Truitner (personal communication).
For a summary of many of the collocational parallels between interrogatives
and imperatives in English, see Katz and Postal (1964).
[6] This does not necessarily imply the exclusion of derivationally-introduced

(ii) In English and many other languages (though perhaps not all languages), there is, in addition to the universal process of subordinate identity deletion, a related process of superordinate identity deletion, which effects the optional deletion of generic heads in constructions such as (*the one*) *who came*, (*the thing*) *what/which I saw*, etc. (cf. Sanders 1967).

(iii) There is a principle (presumably universal) whereby the structures associated with the meanings "I tell you" and "You tell me" may, when not subordinate, be either non-extraposed from their immediately subordinate verb or else assigned a null phonological representation.

(iv) In English and certain other Germanic languages at least there is an obligatory rule of VERB-RAISING which interposes an immediately subordinate verb into the most superordinate clause of a sentence if that clause does not immediately include a verb.

Thus, in accordance with these hypotheses, it will be assumed that all questions are derived from interrogative-free underlying structures, and that any reduced interrogative such as *Where will John go* will be derived consistently along lines such as the following:

(63) BASE: [John will go someplace] [Tell me (the identity of) that place]
        SUBORDINATION PROCESSES
        [Tell me that place [John will go there]]
        RELATIVE REDUCTION PROCESSES
        [Tell me that place [where [John will go]]]
        SUPERORDINATE (HEAD) DELETION
        [Tell me [where [John will go]]]
        SPEAKER-HEARER SUPPRESSION
        [Where [John will go]]
        VERB-RAISING
        [Where will [John go]]

intermediate elements as markers of questions or even of semantically-interpretable non-generic interrogative elements in the underlying representation of particular sub-sentential morphemic constituents such as *question, ask, wonder*, etc. All that is really being excluded by (i) is the use of interrogation as a semantically significant operator or predicate signifying that the structure in construction with it has the property of being questioned.

Given the general theory of question-formation sketched roughly here, every simple, or truncated, question will necessarily undergo all of the general relativization processes undergone by non-interrogative sentences containing relative clauses. All constraints which are applicable with respect to relative formation in declaratives will thus be equally applicable to the formation of interrogative clauses, the latter being explicitly characterized by this theory simply as relative clauses which lack a superficial head or superordinate frame. Bearing this in mind, then, we can simplify the present discussion by dealing only with examples of declarative relativization, with the understanding that everything that is said about these applies equally to the relativization processes underlying all imperative and truncated information questions.

In grammars which allow axiomatic and variable ordering, relativization for languages like English at least has traditionally been accounted for by means of the following major assumptions: (1) a sentence is axiomatically or transformationally included in a noun-phrase as an attributive relative clause in construction with a head noun-phrase; (2) one noun-phrase within the relative clause is identified as the relative constituent if and only if it is referentially and otherwise identical to (or perhaps non-distinct from) the head noun-phrase; (3) the relative constituent is marked as such by the (usually non-axiomatic) inclusion of some particular identifying element or feature (e.g. WH, + REL); (4) the relative constituent (perhaps after also undergoing pronominalization) is assigned an appropriate relative-pronoun phonological representation by lexical rules which make essential reference to its marker, its underlying generic (e.g. pronominal) properties, and its superficial case properties; and (5) the relative constituent is reordered from some position whithin the relative clause to a position immediately following its head.

Now, first of all, it is immediately evident that four of these five assumptions have nothing whatever to do with the ordering or re-ordering of any constituents. These assumptions (1-4) are thus equally compatible with either the axiomatic or the derivational specification of ordering and are entirely consistent with the as-

sumption of invariant derivational ordering as well as with its contradiction. If it is assumed that these traditional assumptions are at least approximately correct, then, rules which express these assumptions will necessarily appear in some form or other in all adequate grammars regardless of their metatheoretical differences with respect to constituent ordering. Moreover, it is quite clear that these rules will be essentially identical in grammars governed by all possible combinations of ordering and reordering constraints, and will differ in fact only with respect to the presence or absence of specifications of ordering between the relevant constants and variables in their structural descriptions and products, along with certain minor differences in abbreviation. If it could be shown then that the explanatory functions of the Complex NP Constraint can be effectively achieved with respect to the application of one of these rules — each of which is equally compatible with invariant and with variable ordering — then it would follow that this constraint is not even ACCIDENTALLY dependent on the existence of reordering and that it is thus entirely consistent — in fact as well as in principle — with the metatheoretical requirement of invariant derivational ordering. We will now show that this is actually the case, not only for ONE of the order-irrelevant assumptions about relative-formation, but for at least TWO of them.

Thus, ignoring lexicalization, and adopting the explanatorily more valuable assumption that relative clauses are included in nominals not axiomatically but by an optional subordination transformation applied to structures which also underlie their coordinative paraphrases, we may assume the following approximate and illustratively somewhat over-specific formulations of the basic rules of relativization in grammars governed by the assumption of axiomatic ordering. All rules are specified as mirror-image conflations, since different axiomatic and derived orderings would presumably be postulated for languages with superficially pre-nominal relatives (e.g. Chinese, Japanese) and for those with post-nominal relatives (e.g. English, Thai). Rule (64iii) is essentially identical to a mirror-image generalization of the schematic "Relative Clause Formation" rule which Ross assumes for the explicit

purpose of illustrating the applicability of his Complex NP Constraint (Ross 1967: 118).

(64) RELATIVE CLAUSE FORMATION IN ORDERED BASE GRAMMARS

(i) SUBORDINATION (optional, mirror-image)

$$\underbrace{_s[U}_{1} \& \underbrace{_{NP}[W]}_{2} \& \underbrace{X]}_{3} \& \underbrace{_s[Y \& _{NP}[W] \& Z]}_{4} \rightarrow 1 \, _{NP}[2 \& 4] \, 3 \, \emptyset$$

(ii) RELATIVE-MARKING (AND PRONOMINALIZATION) (mirror-image)

$$\underbrace{[U \& _{NP}[_{NP}[W] \& _s[Y}_{1} \& \underbrace{_{NP}[W]}_{2} \& \underbrace{Z]] \& X]}_{3} \rightarrow 1 \begin{bmatrix} 2 \\ + \text{REL} \\ + \text{PRO} \end{bmatrix} 3$$

(iii) RELATIVE EXTRAPOSITION AND ORDERING (mirror-image)

$$\underbrace{[U \& _{NP}[_{NP}[W]}_{1} \& \underbrace{_s[Y}_{2} \& \underbrace{_{NP}[W]}_{3} \& \underbrace{Z]]}_{4} \& \underbrace{X]}_{5} \rightarrow 1 \, _s[3 \& 2 \, \emptyset \, 4] \, 5$$

It is clear that if the Complex NP Constraint is interpreted as an analysis-constraint, as in (56), the constraint is violable with respect to rules (64i) and (64ii), as well as with respect to (64 iii). This is because the substring $[_{NP}[W] \& [Y \& _{NP}[W] \& Z]]$, which occurs in the product descriptions of (i) and (iii) and in both the domain and product descriptions of (ii), will be either determinably analyzable or determinably not analyzable as one of the excluded extrapositional structures of (56). More precisely the constraint will exclude the application of any of these rules to any string which can be analyzed as either of the extrapositional structures of (56), including the special case where the structures in that string which are analyzed as the extraposed (D) and interposed (C) of its (56) analysis are also respectively analyzed as the first and second $_{NP}[W]$ of its $[_{NP}[W] \& [Y \& _{NP}[W] \& Z]]$ analysis. It also appears that the derivational formulation of the Complex NP Constraint (54) can be generalized in such a way as to be similarly applicable

with respect to all three of the ordered relativization rules (64i-iii). It also appears likely that this multiple applicability will be preserved when the Complex NP Constraint is ultimately reduced to some more general principle governing the possible scope and bounding of all variables in terms of the constituency or "rank" of their associated constants. For present purposes, however, it suffices that there is at least one formulation of the constraint which is applicable to rules other than Relative Extraposition (iii). It should be noted, moreover, that even if we were to adopt the less productive assumption that relative clauses are included in nominals axiomatically rather than by transformation, it would still be the case that the Complex NP Constraint is applicable with respect to Relative-Marking as well as Relative-Extraposition. And even if we were to collapse Marking and Extraposition into one conflated rule, it would still be the case that the constraint would be applicable to EACH of the elementary subrules comprising the conflation. Also, of course, if there is any motivation for pronominalizing relative nominals, there is clearly no reason to pronominalize them by a special rule (as in 64ii) since they satisfy the GENERAL conditions for NON-RELATIVE pronominalization as well. If relatives are pronominalized then, and if they are pronominalized in the simplest and most general way, there will be a fourth rule — namely, pronominalization — with respect to which the Complex NP Constraint would also be applicable. And this rule, of course, cannot POSSIBLY be conflated with Relative-Extraposition, since it must apply also to structures which contain no relative clauses at all.

Thus the Complex NP Constraint does not depend on the existence of reordering rules even in ordered-base grammars, since its intended filtering function can be adequately achieved with respect to well-motivated non-reordering rules which play an essential role in the derivation of all relative constructions by such grammars.

For grammars which observe the Unordered Base and Invariant Order Constraints, the processes of Subordination and Relative-Marking will be specified by rules which are quite similar to the corresponding mirror-image conflations (64i and 64ii) required in

axiomatic-order grammars. Although a REordering of the relative constituent is obviously unnecessary in unordered-base grammars and neither necessary nor possible in those which also observe the Invariant Order Constraint, it is reasonable to assume that such grammars will include a rule of Relative Extraposition which would also closely parallel to the conflated rule (iii) of the ordered-base grammars. The non-universal rules for Relative Ordering will almost certainly be properly subsumed by more general rules for the ordering of all heads and attributes; for present purposes, though, we can consider these as separate rules which apply to the products of the presumably universal rule of relative extraposition intrinsically prior to the application of all general rules for the ordering of superficial clause constituents of the sort discussed previously.[7] For all grammars governed by the metatheoretical assumption of invariant derivational ordering, then, we may assume the following approximate formulations of the basic rules of relativization:

(65)   RELATIVE   CLAUSE   FORMATION   IN   UNORDERED   BASE
       GRAMMARS

       (i)   SUBORDINATION (optional)

$$_S[X, \, _{NP}[W]], \, _S[Y, \, _{NP}[W]]$$
$$\underset{1 \quad 2}{} \quad \underset{3}{} \quad \rightarrow [1, \, _{NP}[2, 3]]$$

---

[7]   The motivation for positing the extraposition of the relative from its clause is questionable, however, for ordered-base and unordered-base grammars alike. Although in Ross's interpretation of the Complex NP Constraint, the assumption of relative extraposition plays a vital role in the constraint's applicability with respect to relative constructions, he provides no independent justification for this assumption at all. In unordered-base grammars it is possible that motivation for relative extraposition might be found in terms of the general application of ordering rules, e.g. if there is a general rule that in any construction whose immediate constituents are a nominal and a clause the nominal is ordered before the clause in English, Thai, etc., and after the clause in Chinese, Japanese, etc. For ordered-base grammars, however, it is difficult to imagine any empirical basis for choosing between the assumption of extraposition and marginal reordering of relatives and the simple assumption of marginal reordering alone.

(ii) RELATIVE-MARKING (AND PRONOMINALIZATION)

$$\underset{1}{[X, \,_{NP}[[W], \,_{S}[Y, \,_{NP}[W]]]]} \quad \underset{2}{\rightarrow 1,} \begin{bmatrix} 2 \\ REL \\ PRO \end{bmatrix}$$

(iii) RELATIVE EXTRAPOSITION

$$\underset{1}{_{NP}[NP, \,_{S}[[REL], \,\underset{2}{X]]}} \quad \underset{3}{\rightarrow 1, \,_{S}[2, \,_{S}[3]]}$$

(iv) RELATIVE ORDERING[8]

$$\underset{1}{[NP, \,_{S}[[REL], \,\underset{2}{X]]}} \quad \underset{3}{\rightarrow} \begin{Bmatrix} 1 \,\&\, 2 \,\&\, 3 \,/\text{ENGLISH}, \dots \\ 3 \,\&\, 2 \,\&\, 1 \,/\text{JAPANESE}, \dots \end{Bmatrix}$$

As a constraint on regrouping, as in (55), the Complex NP Constraint will clearly serve to restrict the applicability of (65iii) in such a manner as to precisely achieve the intended filtering func-

---

[8] An adequate treatment of the facts about ordering here would clearly have to take account of the mirror-image relations which hold with respect to the superficial orderings of heads and attributes in different natural languages. It would be a simple matter, of course, to formulate a convention for the mirror-image conflation of ordering rules whereby the sequential application of the sub-rules is determined by the form of the conflation itself. Thus, for example, we might adopt the convention that any rule of the form (a) is to be expanded into the ordered sequence of rules (b) followed by (c):

(a) $1, 2, \dots n \rightarrow 1 \,\&\, 2 \,\&\, \dots n$
(b) $1, 2, \dots n \rightarrow 1 \,\&\, 2 \,\&\, \dots \,\&\, n$
(c) $n, \dots 2, 1 \rightarrow n \,\&\, \dots 2 \,\&\, 1$

Given this convention, one of the product descriptions of (iii) could be suppressed. Since input descriptions of ordering rules are always predictable from their output descriptions, rule (iii) could then be reduced simply to

(iv') $\begin{Bmatrix} [NP \,\&\, [[REL] \,\&\, [X]]] \,/\, \text{ENGLISH}, \dots \\ /\, \text{JAPANESE}, \dots \end{Bmatrix}$

The problem with all of this, however, is that we still lack empirically-based criteria for determining WHICH sub-rule should be suppressed, or even WHICH of any number of alternative systems of conflation is correct.

Rules (iv) and (iv') are dubious in other respects as well; for example, they specify the relative ordering of THREE constituents (which are possibly not even mutual sisters), while all motivated ordering rules known thus far apply only to PAIRS of sister constituents.

tion of Ross's linear version of the constraint. The same function is also achieved with respect to the rules of unordered relativization if the Complex NP Constraint is interpreted as a constraint on analysis rather than on restructuring. Thus as a constraint on analysis, we may recall, the Complex NP Constraint can be formulated as

(66) *Rule: ... D ..., $_{NP}[NP, _S[X, C]]$, ...

This constraint is clearly violable with respect to each of the three unordered relativization rules (65i-iii), since each of these rules makes essential reference to representations which it would be logically possible but empirically inappropriate to analyze as (66):

(67) (i)

... → $_S[X, _{NP}[_{NP}[\underline{W}], _S[\underline{\quad Y, \quad} _{NP}[W] \quad] \quad]]$
      $\underline{\quad\quad... D \quad..._{NP}[NP, [X, \quad C \quad] \quad]} ...$

      (ii)

$[X, [_{NP}[\underline{W}], _S[\underline{\quad Y, \quad} _{NP}[W]] \quad] \quad] → ...$
$\underline{\quad... D \quad... [NP, [X, \quad C \quad] \quad]} ...$

      (iii)

$_{NP}[NP, _S[\underline{\quad\quad X, \quad} [REL] \quad] \quad] → ...$
$\underline{\quad... D \quad..._{NP}[NP, _S[X, \quad C \quad] \quad]} ...$

The constraint will thus effectively function to prevent the proper application of any of these three rules of relative formation to any of an infinite set of structures such as (68a) whose surface structures (such as (68b)) are both ungrammatical and derivable only by the violation of this constraint:

(68) (a)

$[[DOG, [[BOY [BOY \underline{CHASING DOG}]], LAUGHING]],$
$\underline{\quad... D \quad... [NP, [\quad\quad X, \quad\quad C]]} ... \quad\quad BARKING]$

      (b) *The dog that the boy that was chasing was laughing
           was barking.

It has thus been shown that reordering is neither necessary nor

sufficient for the most general effective formulation of the Complex
NP Constraint, and that the explanatory functions of this constraint
can be achieved in an entirely principled way by means of grammars
which also observe the Invariant Order Constraint.

4

TEST III: THE CROSSOVER CONSTRAINT

We will turn now to a further test of the constraint-compatibility of Invariant Ordering with respect to the more challenging case of coreferential associativity and Postal's Crossover Principle. This principle, which Postal (1971) formulates as a constraint against derivational changes in the relative order of certain coreferential nominals, is intended to account for a vast number of particular facts about the grammaticality and ungrammaticality of sentences containing anaphoric pronouns and their antecedents.

Thus, for example, any adequate grammar must presumably account in some way for the grammaticality or acceptability contrasts revealed in data such as the following:

(69) (a) Lucifer scratched Gabriel
      (b) Gabriel was scratched by Lucifer
      (c) Lucifer scratched himself
      (d) *Lucifer was scratched by himself[1]

[1] Postal recognizes the fact that sentences such as this are obviously not un grammatical in the same sense as sentences such as
   (a) *He/Himself scratched Lucifer
   (b) *He/Himself was scratched by Lucifer
   (c) *Lucifer was scratched Gabriel
   (d) *Gabriel were scratched by Lucifer

He also acknowledges the central role of stressing in determining the effect of greater or lesser deviance in sentences containing anaphoric constituants, but he does not explore the possibility of EXPLAINING all purported crossover phenomena in terms of stressing processes rather than processes of ordering or reordering. That this avenue of explanation is worthy of serious investigation is shown by data such as the following, where primary clause stress is signified by capitalization:

(70) (a) Cleopatra talked to Lucifer about Gabriel
      (b) Cleopatra talked about Gabriel to Lucifer
      (c) Cleopatra talked to herself about Gabriel
      (d) Cleopatra talked about Gabriel to herself[2]
      (e) Cleopatra talked to Lucifer about himself
      (f) *Cleopatra talked about Lucifer to himself

It is evident from data of this sort that, while alternations in the
relative order of referentially distinct nominals in multiple-case
sentences are normally equivalent in both meaning and grammaticality, in the case of referentially-identical nominals one of the
expected orderings is fully grammatical (e.g. Agent before Patient,
To-phrase before About-phrase) while the other is not (e.g. Patient

---

    (e)   Gabriel was scratched by ELIZABETH, but Lucifer was scratched by
          HIMSELF/by JOSHUA
    (f) *Gabriel was BITTEN by Elizabeth, but Lucifer was SCRATCHED by
          himself/by Joshua
    (g) *GABRIEL was scratched by Elizabeth, but LUCIFER was scratched
          by himself/by Joshua
    (h) What did Lucifer DO to himself/Joshua? Lucifer SCRATCHED
          himself/Joshua
    (i) *What was Lucifer/Joshua DONE (to) by himself/Lucifer?
          Lucifer/Joshua was SCRATCHED by himself/Lucifer

However, since our primary purpose here is not to explain Postal's crossover
data but simply to show that reordering is not necessary for any such explanation, we will ignore stressing and stress-dependent ordering processes for the
most part, and will attempt to view the phenomena in question from Postal's
own viewpoint as much as possible.

[2] Sentence (70d), like (69d), varies in acceptability according to differences in
the location of primary stress, and thus according to the properties of its
adjacent clauses. Thus, for my dialect at least, (70d) is acceptable with primary
stress on either *Cleopatra* or *herself*, but it is unacceptable if the stress is on
talked and marginally acceptable if the stress is on *Gabriel*. This is explainable,
it seems, in terms of the grammaticality or ungrammaticality of the types of
adjacent sentences which determine these differences in stress location:

    (a) WHO talked about Gabriel to herself? CLEOPATRA talked about
          Gabriel to herself
    (b) WHO did Cleopatra talk about Gabriel to? Cleopatra talked about
          Gabriel to HERSELF
    (c) *WHAT did Cleopatra DO about Gabriel to herself? Cleopatra
          TALKED about Gabriel to herself
    (d) ?WHO did Cleopatra talk about to herself? Cleopatra talked about
          GABRIEL to herself

before Agent, About-phrase before To-phrase). It is thus necessary not only to exclude a large number of particular orderings of coreferential nominals, but also to provide some explanation of the fact that the ordering of coreferential nominals is generally more restricted than that of nominals that are referentially-distinct.

Postal proposes to do this in a manner which would perhaps appear to be quite simple and natural in the context of variable-order grammars. His account is based on the assumptions (1) that for at least some pairs of alternately ordered multiple-nominal structures, one ordering is derivationally prior to, or more basic than, the other, the latter structure being derivable only by a trans-formational reordering of the constituents of the former structure; (2) that the basic order postulated for any particular set of con-stituents will correspond to the grammatical superficial order of those constituents when some or all of them are coreferential; and (3) that there is a universal constraint (the Crossover Principle) to the effect that the relative order of associated coreferential nominals must be derivationally invariant.

Assumptions (1) and (2) are incompatible with the Invariant Order Constraint, of course, but it is only if these assumptions are accepted that the order-dependent Crossover Principle can possibly achieve its intended discrimination function. Thus, al-though the Crossover Principle itself is entirely consistent with the Invariant Order Constraint and could be viewed merely as one of its special cases, it is only if SOME nominal orderings are NOT invariant that the invariance of coreferential nominal ordering could be used to account for the fact that the superficial orderings of the latter are MORE RESTRICTED than those of other nominals. The Invariant Order Constraint and Postal's Crossover Theory cannot both be correct, then, and in order to maintain the correctness of the Invariant Order Constraint it would be necessary to show that all significant facts that can be accounted for by Postal's theory can also be accounted for with equal or greater generality by a theory that is entirely consistent with the Invariant Order Constraint.

As in the case of other proposed constraints on reordering, there are a number of general and more or less *a priori* reasons for believing that the explanatory functions of the Crossover Principle can be more appropriately achieved by constraints on the grouping and ordering of constituents rather than on their reordering. A number of these considerations have already been discussed in the previous chapter in connection with the Complex NP Constraint and need not be restated here. Two points that have been previously alluded to, however, appear to be especially relevant to the case of the proposed Crossover Principle. These are worth noting again, however, as evidence that, REGARDLESS of the existence or non-existence of reordering, the Crossover Principle CANNOT be a constraint on reordering. The first point, which is strictly suggestive, concerns the essential function of order-independent grouping conditions in any possible formal expression of any proposed re-ordering constraint; the second point, which appears to be demonstrative in the case of the Crossover Principle, is that any rule-operational formulation of a reordering constraint will always be insufficient to exclude whatever the constraint is intended to exclude. But in this case, if the Crossover Principle is NOT formulated as an operational constraint, i.e. if it is a constraint on analysis or derivational co-occurrence, then it appears that it would also be incapable of achieving its intended function.

The fact that every purported general reordering constraint proposed thus far makes essential use of order-independent constituency relations is sufficient, I believe, to make one suspect that the references to ordering and reordering by these constraints are accidental to their intended explanatory functions and are necessitated only by the empirically unmotivated assumption that underlying structures are ordered. For if grammatical theories really needed to include the power of imposing constraints on the RE-ORDERING of constituents, we would naturally expect to find at least ONE empirically-defensible instance of a PURE constraint on reordering, i.e. a constraint which prohibits some change in the relative order of two constituents REGARDLESS OF their relative grouping or constituency relations. Pure reordering constraints of

this sort are LOGICALLY quite possible, of course, and artificial languages could readily be constructed which would observe any number of pure reordering constraints like those in (71).

(71) (a) No structure including a nominal followed by a verb may be reordered so that the verb precedes the nominal;

(b) A nominal can never be reordered in such a way that it would be immediately preceded and followed by verbs;

(c) The first two constituents of a sentence may not be reordered with respect to each other;

(d) No structure that includes a constituent X to the left of a referentially-identical constituent Y may undergo any reordering such that Y is ordered to the left of X.[3]

Now it is presumably safe to assume that most linguists would agree that there are no natural languages which ever observe any constraints of this sort. Thus, while pure reordering constraints are logically possible, it apparently happens to be a FACT about NATURAL LANGUAGES that they never observe such constraints. Now if this fact is correct, which I believe it is, then it is an empirically significant fact about natural languages which cannot POSSIBLY be accounted for by any theory of language which includes or permits the inclusion of any constraint on reordering. For if there are constraints that refer only to grouping (which is presumably the case for ANY theory of grammar) and if there are also constraints which refer both to grouping and to reordering, then there would clearly be no reasonable way to exclude the possibility of constraints which refer only to reordering. Actually, of course, the non-existence of pure constraints on reordering in natural languages can be most simply explained as a consequence of the non-existence of ANY grammatical constraints on reordering. But since nothing that is of

---

[3] (71d) is, of course, what the Crossover Principle would be like if it really were a pure reordering constraint.

empirical significance can be wholly unconstrained, the only conceivable explanation for the non-existence of reordering constraints would be the non-existence of reordering.

The claim that there are no pure reordering restrictions on natural languages might be contested, of course, on the grounds that it is based on extremely limited knowledge of an extremely limited subset of the set of all possible languages. However, even if this is granted as a legitimate objection, and even if we were to consider the apparent non-existence of such constraints only an accidental property of certain known languages, it would still be the case that all attempted formulations of constraints making reference to reordering also make extensive essential reference to constituency relations and in most cases are clearly more complex than any functionally equivalent constraint which makes reference ONLY to the constituency relations of unordered structures. In the case of Crossover Principle, the extent of its complexity and dependence on constituency is so great that it would certainly be reasonable to suspect that something is radically wrong here somewhere, and that, in spite of Postal's brilliant effort to accommodate all of the vast array of crossover phenomena which he has brought to light, these phenomena are simply not explainable in terms of the notion of reordering.

There is, of course, no way to decide how complex a scientific explanation has to be before we consider it too complex to be an explanation of anything. Nor is there any way to decide when a given explanatory principle is so restricted in applicability and so dependent on other factors that we come to feel certain that it is incorrect. I can only cite, for consideration in these respects, Postal's most complete formulation of the Crossover Principle (Postal 1971:120, 181). (I have omitted Postal's italicization here and have added my own italicizations for each term or concept that refers solely to the form and constituency or grouping of structures entirely independent of their ordering or reordering):

... we assume the following definitions: 14. (1) *Variable* movement rule (transformation) as in Chapter 13. 14. (2) *Constant* movement rule (transformation) as in Chapter 13. 14. (3) The application path of a

transformation T with respect to a *phrase marker P*: the sequence of *constituents in P* over which a *constituent* is moved by T_i when it applies to *P*.

Consider then the following: 14. (4) An arbitrary movement transformation T with a Structure Index *K*, whose *i*th item is *NP*, and whose operation reorders the *i*th term of proper analyses. 14. (5) The *set* of all *phrase markers S* meeting the condition *K* (that is, having Proper Analyses with respect to *K*.) 14. (6) An arbitrary phrase marker *P* which is a member of *S* and whose Proper Analysis with respect to T has NP_k as its *i*th term ...

Cross-Over VI. Despite the fact that *P* is a member of *S*, T may not apply to *P* if the application path of T with respect to *P* is such that this path contains an NP_j *coreferential* with NP_k and both NP_j and NP_k are *Pronominal Virgins* [i.e. NP's which have not undergone any rule of pronominalization] and either:

(a) T is a *Variable* Movement rule.
(b) T is a *Constant* Movement rule and NP_k and NP_j are both *Clause Mates* [i.e. each is included in every clause that the other is included in] and *Peers* [i.e. NP's whose paths to the same S are free of NP's that don't dominate S's].

Referring to the preceding explicit formulation of the Crossover Principle, we may now proceed to the second general argument, which shows that it is impossible in principle for the intended explanatory function of this constraint to be achieved in any reasonable way by means of a constraint on reordering regardless of whether such a constraint is imposed an transformational operations, on rule-analyses, or on derivational co-occurrences. As can be seen from the above quotation, Postal explicitly formulates the Crossover Principle as an operational constraint, and he consistently refers to it in this way in his informal discussions as well. In order to interpret it as an operational constraint, however, Postal is forced to allow an exceptionally powerful metatheoretical device to be added to the already excessively powerful arsenal of linguistic theory. This is the otherwise quite unmotivated device of rule-output determination of rule-applicability.

The following principle appears to have been generally accepted thus far as an explicit or implicit metaconstraint on all con zmporary explanatory theories of grammar:

(72)   Given any Theory of Grammar, T, any grammatical rule, R, which is well-formed according to T, and any arbitrary string of symbols, S, the ordered triple (T, R, S) FULLY DETERMINES the APPLICABILITY or NON-APPLICABILITY of R to S, by FULLY DETERMINING a PRODUCT, or OUTPUT, string S', where the non-identity of S and S' formally characterizes the APPLICABILITY of R to S, and the identity of S and S' formally characterizes the (optional or obligatory) NON-APPLICABILITY of R to S.

In other words, it has traditionally been required that rules and inputs determine outputs, i.e. that each line of a linguistic derivation must follow necessarily given only the immediately preceding line, some grammatical rule, and the constraints and rules of inference of some governing metatheory.

Postal's formulation of the Crossover Principle clearly violates this metaconstraint, since its essential concept of "the application path of T with respect to P" is determinable only by the COMPARISON of P with P', the product of the APPLICATION of T to P. To put it somewhat metaphorically, this form of the Crossover Principle can be applied only if we first ALLOW a rule to apply and then COMPARE the derivational line resulting from such application with the immediately preceding line to determine whether or not there is any improper "crossing" relation between coreferential NP's in the two derivational lines; finally, if there IS such a relation between the two lines, the last line is erased and we proceed to some other rule. It is quite possible, of course, that evidence for the necessity of such "scouting" of subsequent lines of derivations might ultimately be found. In the meantime, however, it is appropriate to hold to the narrower constraints of the traditional principle of output-independent applicability-determination and to be highly sceptical of any proposal which requires the abandonment of this principle.

It is also evident that, although Postal's formulation is intended to restrict the applicability of SINGLE RULES, it is actually expressed as a special type of DERIVATIONAL CO-OCCURRENCE constraint,

namely one which prohibits the co-occurrence of certain structures
in IMMEDIATELY ADJACENT lines of any derivation. This adjacency
restriction is neither necessary nor sufficient, however, for any of
the intended explanatory purposes of the Crossover Principle. This
follows, as we have shown in connection with the Complex NP
Constraint, from the fact that the PRODUCT of any SINGLE RE-
ORDERING RULE can always also be effected by an indefinitely large
number of indefinitely large SETS of reordering rules or combinations of indefinitely separated iteration, grouping, ordering, and
deletion rules. Thus while Postal's constraint would prevent the
DIRECT derivation of (73b) from (73a) by application of the SINGLE
rule (74), it cannot prevent any number of otherwise entirely possible INDIRECT derivations of (b) from (a) by means of entirely
normal SETS of rules such as (75) or (76):

(73) (a) $[[Lucifer, \text{AGENT}][scratched[Lucifer, \text{PATIENT}]]]$
      (b) $[[Lucifer, \text{PATIENT}][was\ scratched\ [by\ Lucifer,$
           $\text{AGENT}]]]$

(74) $[[X, \text{AGENT}]\ \&\ [\text{VERB}\ \&\ [Y, \text{PATIENT}]]]$

$$1 \qquad\qquad 2 \qquad\qquad \rightarrow 3\ \&\ \begin{bmatrix} 2 \\ \text{PASSIVE} \end{bmatrix}\ \&\ 1$$

(75) (i)   PREDICATE FRONTING
            $[X\ \&\ [\text{PREDICATE}]]$
            $\qquad 1 \qquad\quad 2 \qquad\qquad$ —reordering $\rightarrow 2\ \&\ 1$
      (ii) VERB RETRACTION
            $_s[\text{VERB}\ \&\ \text{NOMINAL}\ \&\ X]$
            $\qquad 1 \qquad\quad 2 \qquad\quad 3$ —reordering $\rightarrow 2\ \&\ 1\ \&\ 3$

(76) (i)   VERB ITERATION AND ORDERING
            $[X\ \&\ \text{VERB}\ \&\ Y]$
            $\qquad 1 \qquad 2 \qquad 3 \rightarrow 2\ \&\ 1\ \&\ 2\ \&\ 3$
      (ii) PATIENT ITERATION AND ORDERING
            $[X\ \&\ [\text{PATIENT}]\ \&\ Y]$
            $\qquad 1 \qquad\quad 2 \qquad\quad 3 \rightarrow 2\ \&\ 1\ \&\ 2\ \&\ 3$
      (iii) IDENTITY DELETION
            $[W\ \&\ X\ \&\ Y\ \&\ X\ \&\ Z]$
            $\qquad 1 \quad 2 \quad 3 \quad 4 \quad 5 \rightarrow 1\ \&\ 2\ \&\ 3\ \&\ \emptyset\ \&\ 5$

If the Crossover Principle is interpreted as a derivational co-occurrence constraint, on the other hand, indirect violations would still be possible unless the axiomatic constituency and/or order of every nominal is "carried down" to every derivation of the nominal. For it is only if these axiomatic relations are specified by inherent features of nominals which remain invariant under all transformations that it would be possible to determine for any pair of lines in a derivation whether or not an improper change in axiomatic ordering has been effected. But this would require an entirely *ad hoc* and empirically intolerable expansion of the set of axiomatic elements that are necessary and sufficient for the representation of the underlying structures of all linguistic objects. The expansion, moreover, would have to be unlimited, since there is no upper bound on the number of distinct sequential positions in ordered underlying structures which could be occupied by a nominal which might subsequently occur out of its original sequential position relative to some other coreferential nominal. Thus, since axiomatic inherent elements are, by definition, semantically-interpretable, and since the infinite number of required initial place-features would obviously not be interpretable, these features would presumably have to be introduced by some pre-cyclic transformation, a transformation whose sole function would be to assign a unique sequential order marker to each constituent of any given axioma-tically-ordered structure. But these markers and the rule that assigns them would then be motivated ONLY with respect to their use in identifying possible crossover violations, which certainly cannot be considered sufficient justification for an infinite enlargement of the set of intermediate (uninterpreted) elements of linguistic theories, or for the required DOUBLE specification of axiomatic order (once by axiomatic ordering operators, again by transformationally-introduced initial-order markers), especially when this non-superficial ordering property of linguistic objects is both semantically and phonologically empirically non-significant.

This would appear to leave only the analysis-constraint interpretation as a possible interpretation of the Crossover Principle. But the most natural formulation would then be as a prohibition against

the analysis of any structure with respect to any rule in such a way that any two terms of the rule are analyzed as structures which are coreferential. Although this might ultimately prove to be an essentially correct expression of the principle underlying Postal's various crossover phenomena, it is evident that this principle no longer has ANY relation to ordering or reordering, and is thus fully compatible with the assumption of invariant derivational ordering. In any event, though, this interpretation of the Crossover Principle as an analysis constraint prohibiting coreference to coreferential nominals is not possible in the context of Postal's discussion, since he assumes the existence of a large number of rules (e.g. Reflexivization, Equi-NP Deletion, Pronominalization) which do make reference to coreferential nominals and which would thus be universally non-applicable if this analysis constraint were to be observed. It would thus appear that in his frame of reference there is no natural or effective way at all to achieve the intended functions of the Crossover Principle.

We have suggested several reasons for believing that any formulation of the Crossover Principle as a constraint on reordering will either be inadequate with respect to its intended explanatory functions or else so encumbered with *ad hoc* conditions and powers as to be incompatible with other well-motivated constraints on grammars and theories of grammar. However, it obviously cannot be concluded that the Crossover Principle is incorrect and that the Invariant Order Constraint is consequently still substantiated unless it can be shown that all of the very interesting crossover phenomena which Postal has reported can be adequately accounted for by theories which accept the Invariant Order Condition and thus exclude the possibility of any particular constraint on reordering. To do justice to this task would require the labors of quite a few linguists for quite a few years, particularly in view of the fact that most of Postal's data can properly be said to be presently uninvestigated, and most of the rest presently unexplained. Even by restricting our attention to certain limited aspects of the relatively well-studied problems of active-passive and oblique

nominal alternation, we cannot hope to achieve more than a general indication of the explanatory powers available to invariant-order theories and the promise they hold for the eventual explanation of these and other types of phenomena reported by Postal.

If the Invariant Order Constraint is correct, then all superficial ordering relations must be determined by ordering rules which are defined upon given unordered groupings of given constituents. All restrictions on the relative order of coreferential nominals must thus be explainable in terms of the inherent or derived properties and constituency relations of these nominals and the general ordering rules which are dependent on these properties and relations. Since the characteristic inherent properties of all nominals which observe crossover restrictions are identity of reference and non-identity of function, and since their characteristic derivational property is that one is an anaphoric reduction of the other, it would be natural to begin any investigation of crossover phenomena with an investigation of the relations that hold between function, grouping, anaphora, and ordering in natural languages.

We will first adopt without discussion the traditional and well-motivated assumption that there are non-superficial groupings and that particular groupings of this sort are associated with particular underlying case or functional properties of the constituents which are grouped. It is quite possible that all such groupings can be derived by general transformations defined on the inherent generic properties of axiomatically ungrouped constituents (see, e.g. Fillmore 1966, Sanders 1967), but for present purposes the nature, axiomaticity, and directionality of the dependency between non-superficial grouping and generic properties is irrelevant, as long as there is some stage in every derivation where these groupings and properties are both specified.

We will also assume that in the derivation of every active transitive sentence and every (non-stative) passive sentence there is at least one line which can be analyzed as

(77)   ... [[N, AGENT], [[N, -AGENT], [VERB]]] ...

The ultimate correctness of this assumption is a matter of considerable doubt, of course, since there are a great many important facts about active-passive alternations and other related matters which are still largely unexamined and almost wholly unexplained. Nevertheless, I know of no clear evidence that the assumption is false, and it at least has the advantage of corresponding to what are undoubtedly the two most common conventional treatments of such sentences: (1) as axiomatically simple sentences with Agent Nominal and Predicate as immediate constituents and with the Patient, Dative, Instrument, etc., included in the Predicate; or (2) as axiomatically or derivationally complex sentences where the Agent Nominal is an immediate constituent of the superordinate sentence and the non Agent Nominal and the (axiomatically adjectival or non-transitive) Verb are the immediate constituents of the subordinate sentence, and where the subordinate sentence stands in an essentially predicative relation with respect to the Agent. We will accept this assumption then, and also the presumably reasonable assumption that any conclusions drawn on the basis of examples restricted to sentences with Agents and Patients will hold *mutatis mutandis* for parallel sentences with other types of non-Agent nominals.

The correct surface representation of any active transitive sentence can be derived quite directly from its unordered structure analyzed as (77) by the application of the general ordering rules for major clause constituents discussed previously (Ch. 2), along with the appropriate extraposition, ordering, and lexicalization rules for the sub-constituents of these major constituents. The latter rules will be ignored, as their general properties are quite regular and have no bearing on the present problem.

The general rules for the ordering of clause constituents in English were formulated earlier, it will be recalled, as in (78),

(78)   (1a) $[V, O] \rightarrow [V \& O]$
       (2) $[S, O] \rightarrow [S \& O]$

where the symbols S and O were defined as expository abbreviations for the characteristic properties or grouping relations of all

superficial subjects and complements, respectively. It is now necessary to eliminate these expository devices and express these rules in a more normal and more general form. There are several ways in which this could be done, but it is easiest and also most relevant to the present discussion to begin with a way in which it can NOT be done. This is by simply substituting AGENT and -AGENT for S and O, respectively, in the rules (78). Such substitution would be possible, of course, only if English were a language in which ALL superficial subjects and complements are derived, respectively, from underlying Agents and non-Agents, and in which EVERY underlying Agent and non-Agent is ordered respectively before and after its Verb. But it is obvious that this is not true, since both Agents and non-Agents are sometimes ordered before verbs and sometimes after them, as evidenced by any number of sentences such as

(79) (a) Lucifer scratched Gabriel   (AGENT & VERB & -AGENT)

           Gabriel was scratched by Lucifer   (-AGENT & VERB & AGENT)

    (b) Lucifer wanted power   (-AGENT & VERB & -AGENT)

           Power was given to Lucifer   (-AGENT & VERB & -AGENT)

           Lucifer had a pitchfork   (-AGENT & VERB & -AGENT)

    (c) Lucifer danced   (AGENT & VERB)

           Lucifer suffered   (-AGENT & VERB)

Actually, of course, there are NO natural languages in which the ordering of nominals is fully predictable from their UNDERLYING case properties, or their underlying case properties from their ordering. This is shown by the fact that every language has at least SOME of the following types of order-alternations, alternations with respect to which all significant semantic and syntactic properties and co-occurrence relations are apparently invariant and which are thus explainable in a principled way only as the result of alter-

nate derivations from the same underlying structure and the same underlying configuration of case properties:

(80) (a) *Lucifer* was interested *in pitchforks*
           Pitchforks were interesting *to Lucifer*
      (b) There are no snakes *in Ireland*
           Ireland has no snakes
      (c) *Lucifer* borrowed a trumpet *from Gabriel*
           Gabriel loaned a trumpet *to Lucifer*
      (d) *Louis* came *after Charles*
           After Charles came *Louis*
           Charles came *before Louis*
           Before Louis came *Charles*
           Louis followed *Charles*
           Charles preceded *Louis*
      (e) Phyllis went home *at five o'clock*
           At five o'clock Phyllis went home
      (f) *This door* can't be opened *with an ordinary key*
           An ordinary key can't open *this door*

These examples also suffice to demonstrate that, while SOME nominal orderings can be correctly predicted from the presence or absence of overt extraposed lexical MANIFESTATIONS of their underlying case properties (80a, b, c, f), there will also be many orderings which can NOT be predicted in this way (cf. 80d, e). Since the ordering of nominals is not fully predictable on the basis of either their underlying case properties or the superficial manifestations of these case properties, it follows that if nominal ordering is predictable at all, which it obviously is, then it must be predictable on the basis of the GROUPING of the nominals relative to other constituents of their clauses.

It is clear, though, that the groupings which ordering rules are defined on cannot always be identical to the axiomatic grouping of the constituents that are ordered, for if there were no derivational alternations in grouping, there would be no way to account for the fact that there are alternations in ordering, to say nothing of the vast number of other types of alternation which also depend

on the possibility of derivational regrouping. It is thus necessary to accept the conventional assumption that there is a phonologically-initial grouping of constituents in all phonetically-terminated derivations, and that this grouping is not necessarily identical to that specified in any preceding line of the derivation. More precisely we are assuming that the set of possible formula-types, or statement-forms, for all grammars of natural languages includes the statement-form

(81) $[W], [X, Y] = [W, X], [Y],$

where W may be null; interpositional and extrapositional association, or regrouping, transformations are thus available as possible derivational rules of any language. It will be noted that regrouping is explicitly defined by this schema as a relation that holds only with respect to unordered constituents; from this and from the fact that constituents and constituency relations are invariant under ordering transformations, it follows that any rule which effects a regrouping of constituents relative to each other must necessarily be applied prior to any rule which effects their ordering relative to each other. For present purposes we can make the somewhat stronger but less firmly established assumption that ALL regrouping rules are applied before ANY ordering rule is applied. Thus, along with lexical rules, or simply as a special case of lexicalization,[4] all ordering rules apply in phonetically-directed derivations only after all other non-phonological rules have applied.

Having established the existence and variability of grouping relations and the phonetically-directed derivational precedence of regrouping to ordering, it is clear that if we can now effect the optional regrouping of axiomatic or axiomatically-determined structures of the form

(82) $[[N, AGENT], [[N, -AGENT], [VERB]]]$

---

[4] That is, the special case where the non-phonological and phonological members of a lexical equation are the operators respectively determining the semantically-significant relation of commutative grouping (symbolized by comma) and the phonetically-significant relation of non-commutative ordering (symbolized by ampersand). For further discussion, see Sanders (1972).

into alternate structures of the form

(83) $[[N, \text{-AGENT}], [[N, \text{AGENT}], [\text{VERB}]]]$

it should be possible to reformulate the general ordering rules for clause constituents in such a way that the expository abbreviations "superficial subject" and "superficial object or complement" are replaced respectively by the determinable relations

(84) N of $[N, [V, X]]$ (Superficial Subject)
N_1 of $[[N_1, X], N_2]$ (Superficial Complement)

If we were concerned only with the characterization of unreduced transitive clauses, the case-free grouping-dependent ordering rules for clause constituents in English could be formulated most directly as

(85)   (1a) $[[N, V], N]$
             $1 \quad 2 \quad 3 \;\rightarrow 2 \;\&\; 1, 3 \quad (= V \;\&\; O)$
       (2) $[N, [X, N]]$
             $1 \quad 2 \quad\; \rightarrow 1 \;\&\; 2 \quad\quad (= S \;\&\; O)$

These rules are partially identical and their order of application is empirically significant; they would thus be subject to conflation according to well-motivated general principles. However, there would be no point in doing this without first revising these rules, since all of their formulations thus far fail to account for the ordering of constituents in clauses which lack superficial complements, thereby obscuring the generalization that superficial subjects are ordered pre-predicatively in English not only in unreduced transitive clauses but also in all other clauses. In other words, it is now appropriate to generalize these ordering rules in such a way as to also effect the correct ordering of superficial subjects and non-subjects in simple intransitive sentences such as (86a), as well as in transitive clauses which have undergone complement deletion (86b) or verb deletion (86c):

(86)   (a)   Fish can swim
             Cleopatra was cute
             Every cat is a mammal

(b) Fred hit and Henry kicked the dog

(c) Nicholas drank wine, and Alexander vodka

It will be noted that (85.2) has already been formulated so as to account for the S & O ordering in verbally-reduced clauses as in (86c). Thus the X of (85.2), like all unrestricted variables, may represent null as well as non-null structures. Hence if the structure underlying *Alexander vodka* of (86c) has the pre-ordering form [[ALEXANDER], [[VODKA]]], rule (85.2) will be properly applicable to it:

(87) [[ALEXANDER], [[∅], [VODKA]]]
$$\underbrace{\qquad}_{\substack{N \\ 1}} \quad \underbrace{\qquad}_{\substack{X \qquad N \\ 2}} \qquad \text{—rule (85.2)} \to 1 \,\&\, 2$$

In addition to the use of the unrestricted variable, this treatment clearly depends on the specification and determinability of the double-bracketing of the complement nominal, since without this distinctive predicative grouping, subjects and non-subjects would not be differentiable and thus could ONLY be ordered COMMUTA-TIVELY with respect to each other. It is thus necessary to assume that the brackets enclosing any n-ary construction REMAIN around the resulting m constituents of that construction after the deletion or extraposition of any $n\text{-}m$ of their sister constituents (where $n \neq m$); in other words, for the case under consideration, the product of verb deletion applied to structures of the form [[N], [V]] must be [[N]] and NOT [N].

The metatheoretical principle determining this preservation of bracketing appears to be independently motivated, but it is neither necessary nor possible to adequately justify it here, or to argue for its formulation in one way rather than another. We will thus simply assume what thus far seems to me the most useful expression of this principle, namely the following universal convention for the (obligatory) elimination of bracketing, or grouping relations, from linguistic representations:

(88) BRACKET ELIMINATION CONVENTION: Any string [W [X] Y]
is replaced by the string [W X Y] if and only if X is fully

ordered, i.e. if and only if it is wholly free of commas and every constituent included in it is flanked by ampersands, or by a bounding bracket and an ampersand.

The independently necessary elimination of brackets surrounding null strings will be effected simply as a special case by this convention, since null strings are free of commas and include no constituents, and hence no constituents that are not ordered.

Two implications of this convention require brief mention here. The first is that the adoption of this convention might serve to reduce the theory of cyclic rule application (see Chomsky 1965) as well as many particular restrictions on the relative order of application of different types of grammatical rules to independent metatheoretical principles of a universal theory of grammar. Thus the possibility of cyclic rule applicability starting with innermost constituents follows as a necessary consequence of the fact that (1) all deletion, adjunction, regrouping, and ordering rules depend for their proper application on the existence of distinctively different bracketings of constituents, (2) such rules can thus apply with respect to any string X only if the bracket elimination convention has not yet applied to X, i.e. only if some ordering rules have not yet applied to X, and (3) that for any string [W [X] Y] it is logically possible that X may be fully ordered and hence bracket free while either W or Y or both are not, but it is not possible that [W [X] Y] could be fully ordered while [X] is not fully ordered. Moreover, it is evident that this convention requires that the last rules applied in any cycle must be ordering rules. Since the logical subsequence of ordering to deletion and other transformational processes has been typically found to be EMPIRICALLY well-motivated (see Chapters 2, 3) and to result in simpler and more general explanations than those possible if ordering were to precede these other processes, the bracket elimination convention may appropriately be said to provide some EXPLANATION of all the various particular cases where non-ordering rules are found to be most appropriately applied prior to the application of ordering rules.[5]

---

[5]   Brackets around individual morphemes will not be eliminated until phono-

The second general point about bracket-elimination concerns the distinction between the GROUPING of constituents into constructions and the internal or external IDENTIFICATION, or LABELING,

---

logical rules have effected the complete ordering of all phonological elements in their superficial representations. Prior elimination of morpheme bracketing will be prevented as a consequence of the fact that there are no rules which effect the ordering of minimal non-phonological constituents such as ANIMATE, STATIVE, FEMININE, etc., relative to each other, along with the fact that each lexical rule effects the replacement of an unordered (or partially ordered) structure consisting of such non-phonological elements with another unordered structure consisting of phonological elements such as VOICED, BACK, SYLLABIC, etc. It is thus only after these latter structures have been reduced to fully ordered strings that the bracket-elimination convention can apply. It should be noted, though, that this convention could be permitted to have the effect of eliminating all word, phrase, and clause bracketings prior to the application of any phonological rules. Although some use has traditionally been made of such bracketings with respect to the specification of stress and other prosodic properties of sentences, there is considerable evidence that focal stressing and destressing processes must apply to non-phonological constituents prior to the application of various general syntactic transformations (see, e.g. Gleitman 1965, Sanders 1967). The dependence of ordering on prior specifications of focal stress is most obvious, but, as shown by Gleitman, there are also clear dependency relations between focal stressing and anaphora-formation and coordinative reduction. In general, in fact, it is quite clear that while the patterns of stress distribution among the SYLLABLES of words or phrases are phonologically-predictable, the patterns of stress distribution among the WORDS and PHRASES of sentences are not phonologically predictable at all, but are fully predictable, rather, in terms of the semantic-syntactic properties of associated phrases and clauses. Thus it is reasonable to assume that con-stituent-stress will have been introduced into construction with word and phrase structures before lexicalization applies, and thus that ordinary lexicaliza-tion would effect the derivation of structures like (b) from structures like (a), where capitalization and italicization represent unordered non-phonological and phonological structures, respectively:

   (a) [JOHN, STRESS] & [RAN] & [UP, STRESS] & [BILL, STRESS] & [RAN] & [DOWN, STRESS]

   (b) [*John*, STRESS] & [*ran*] & [*up*, STRESS] & [*Bill*, STRESS] & [*ran*] & [*down*, STRESS]

Subsequent phonological rules will then distribute the phonological counter-parts of STRESS downward into appropriate subordinate constituents of their constructions, thereby eliminating the unordered relations between STRESS and other constituents and hence allowing for the elimination of the brackets around these constructions. Although many problems of detail remain, it thus would appear that the bracket-elimination convention is entirely adequate for phonological as well as syntactic purposes.

of these constructions. Constructions may be named or otherwise identified in a number of different ways, of course, but it is quite clear that regardless of what system of identification is employed the existence and transformational changes of the BRACKETING of any construction are logically independent of the existence and changes of the NAMES associated with that construction.

The independence of naming and the object named is most obvious in the case of all systems of arbitrary category-naming of the sort represented by nearly all structuralist grammars and all forms of transformational grammar which allow for the existence of categorial elements and labeled brackets. Thus for grammars of this sort it would be possible, for example, to assign the arbitrary name "Sentence" to underlying constructions whose immediate constituents are a Nominal and a Predicate, and to EITHER eliminate OR preserve the association of this name with the construction resulting from the deletion or extraposition of either of these constituents, or from the interposition into the construction of one or more other constituents. For such grammars then it is clear that the derivational "destruction" of structure, specifically of the ordinary "tree-pruning" sort (see, e.g. Ross 1966), can only be determined by PARTICULAR principles governing the preservation or elimination of PARTICULAR LABELS on the brackets enclosing transformationally altered constructions. Such systems thus allow for the elimination or preservation of a label on the SAME brackets under different conditions, as, for example, if a denominalized clause were to be allowed to preserve its sentencehood, while a deverbalized one were stipulated to lose it:

(89) (a) $_S[[N][V]]$—rule n → $_S[[V]]$ (no pruning)
      (b) $_S[[N][V]]$—rule m → $_S[[N]]$—pruning→$[N]$

Bracket preservation and elimination is also independent of identification for those more narrowly constrained theories which employ non-arbitrary and axiomatically non-categorial systems for the identification of constructions. (See Chomsky 1970, Sanders 1967.) Thus, for example, given a non-categorial unlabeled bracketing system such as that proposed in Sanders (1967), all possible

identification or naming of linguistic structures is determined by the metatheoretical principle,

(90) The representation (x) identifies, names, and refers to the set of representations $(R_1, R_2, \ldots R_n)$ such that for any R_i, R_i is analyzable as $[x, y, [Z]]$, where:

(a) x is a non-null string of (sister) immediate constituents of $[x, y, [Z]]$ such that each of these constituents is analyzable as $[a [W]]$ where W is any (possibly null) string and a is a single non-null constant element included in the (finite) set of possible linguistic elements specified by the governing general theory of grammar;

(b) y is either null or a string of immediate constituents analyzable in the same way as x;

(c) Z is any null or non-null string.

According to this principle, any construction can be named or identified by any one or more of its GENERIC properties, i.e. by those SINGLE ELEMENTS which are IMMEDIATELY INCLUDED in the construction. Thus, for example, if we assume that N and V are linguistic elements, then the structural description (91a) will be satisfied by the representations (91a-d) but will not be satisfied by (91e):

(91) (a) $X[N]Y$

(b) $X[N, [V, N]]Y$

(c) $X[N, [V]]Y$

(d) $X[N, [N]]Y$

(e) $*X[[N], V]Y$

Thus it is only the deletion or extraposition of the generic properties, or head, of a construction which can affect its identification, the preservation or elimination of attributes and their bracketing being inherently incapable of affecting any change in the naming or identification of the construction.

Given some system of analysis of this sort, then, along with the universal Bracket Elimination Convention (88), we may now reformulate (85 1a, 2) as follows:

(92) $\begin{array}{cc} [\text{N}, [\text{X}]] \\ 1 \quad 2 \end{array} \rightarrow \begin{cases} 2 \ \& \ 1/[\text{N}, \underline{\quad}] & (=1\text{a}) \\ 1 \ \& \ 2 & (=2) \end{cases}$

It will be noted that if ordering rules are universally constrained to apply cyclically from innermost groupings outwards, then the unmarked, or context-suppressed, or properly-included sub-rule of (92) will subsume the ordered sequence of rules (1b) and (2) which are required for the ordering of clause constituents in Japanese-type languages (see Ch. 2). Thus for a universal grammar for the universe of English and Japanese, a single conflated rule will suffice for the specification of all orderings of major clause constituents in these languages:

(93) NOMINAL ORDERING

$\begin{array}{cc} [\text{N}, [\text{X}]] \\ 1 \quad 2 \end{array} \rightarrow \begin{cases} 2 \ \& \ 1/\text{ENGLISH}, [\text{N}, \underline{\quad}] \\ 1 \ \& \ 2 \end{cases}$

For present purposes, we may consider this to be a correct expression of the general principles governing the ordering of nominal clause constituents for at least this universe of languages.

Given this rule and the various independent assumptions and constraints discussed above, all that remains now for the explanation of crossover phenomena of the active-passive type is the determination of principles which allow for the derivation of pre-ordering structures of the forms (94a-b) while preventing the derivation of any structures of the form (94c-d):

(94) (a) [[N, X], [[N, -X], [V]]]

      (b) [[N, X, -ANAPHORIC], [[N, X, ANAPHORIC, -AGENT], [V]]]

      (c) *[[N, X, ANAPHORIC], [[N, X, -ANAPHORIC, AGENT], [V]]]

      (d) *[[N, X, -ANAPHORIC], [[N, X, ANAPHORIC, AGENT], [V]]].

Thus the nominal ordering rule (93) will correctly derive structures such as (95a) and (95b) from (94a) and (94b), respectively, but would

also derive the ungrammatical structures (95c) and (95d) from (94c) and (94d) if these latter structures were available at the stage where (93) applies:

(95)　(a)　[Lucifer] & [[scratched] & [Gabriel]]
　　　　　　[Gabriel] & [[was scratched] & [by Lucifer]]
　　　(b)　[Lucifer] & [[scratched] & [himself]]
　　　(c)　*[He/Himself] & [[was scratched] & [by Lucifer]]
　　　(d)　*[Lucifer] & [[was scratched] & [by himself]].

We must now consider certain general aspects of the process of anaphoric reduction and ordering. It can readily be seen, first, that all sentences such as (95c) violate a very general and well-known principle governing the relative order of anaphoric constituents and their antecedents in all languages: namely, that a constituent which includes an anaphoric expression must be ordered AFTER the (mutually non-subordinate) SISTER constituent which includes its antecedent. Thus, as has been observed by Langacker (1969), Ross (1969), and others, it is generally the case that a surface structure is well-formed only if all antecedents precede their pronouns and/or are not commanded by them. (X commands Y if and only if X is [non-subordinately] included in a sentence which includes Y.)

For grammars which permit axiomatic ordering of constituents the general requirement that antecedents precede and/or are not commanded by their anaphoric reductions has traditionally been expressed by means of two distinct and mutually non-reducible complementary conditions. Thus regardless of whether the anaphoric ordering restriction is imposed as an *ad hoc* condition on the application of particular pronominalization rules, as in Ross (1969), or as an *ad hoc* well-formedness condition on surface structures including coreferential nominals, as suggested, for example, by Lakoff (1968), it is necessary to allow for EITHER of the relative orderings

(96)　(a)　... [N, X, -ANAPHORIC] & Y & [N, X,
　　　　　　ANAPHORIC] ...

(b)   ... $_S$[W & $_S$[U & [N, X, ANAPHORIC] & Z] &
Y & [N, X, -ANAPHORIC]] ...

It is important to note that these two anaphoric configurations are
not conflatable, even if the powerful mirror-image conflation
convention is metatheoretically available — in fact, the mirror-
image of (96a) is universally ungrammatical. But even more important than this is the fact that these conditions are entirely
ad hoc. Thus any grammar or theory of grammar which INCOR-
PORATES them thereby becomes inherently incapable of generating
any EXPLANATION of the fact that precisely these two anaphoric
configurations are the primary grammatical configurations found in
all known natural languages.

There would appear to be only one way for ordered base theories
to escape from this explanatory *cul-de-sac*; namely, by the reduction of all anaphoric ordering restrictions to a single derivational
form of Postal's Crossover Principle. Thus, although Postal himself says nothing about the possibility of such a reduction, it can
readily be seen that if there were a single pre-cyclic rule of anaphora-
formation in ordered-base grammars, it could be expressed in a
simple one-directional condition-free form, such as

(97)   X & [N, W] & Y & [N, W] & Z
       1   2   3   4   5 → 1 2 3 $\left[\begin{array}{c} 4 \\ \text{ANAPHORIC} \end{array} \right]$ 5

Since all reordering processes would be applicable to anaphoric
configurations with antecedents before their pronouns, a constraint
against the derivational reordering of mutually-non-subordinative
antecedents and pronouns relative to each other would effectively
prohibit all improper derivations such as (98) while allowing the
alternate derivations of (99):

(98)   (a)   Lucifer scratched Bertha and Gabriel kissed her →
             *Gabriel kissed her and Lucifer scratched Bertha
       (b)   Cleopatra admired herself →
             *She/Herself was admired by Cleopatra
(99)   (a)   Lucifer scratched Bertha after Gabriel kissed her →
             After Gabriel kissed her, Lucifer scratched Bertha

(b) Cleopatra admired the man who loved her →
     The man who loved her was admired by Cleopatra

There are numerous obstacles in this path towards the explanation of anaphoric ordering restrictions, however, many of which
appear at present to be wholly insurmountable. It suffices to merely
mention the widely-observed fact that there is a THIRD anaphoric
configuration for sentences such as (99a),

(99) (a') After Gabriel kissed Bertha, Lucifer scratched her

which cannot be accounted for at all if both of the others are accounted for and if pronominalization is both pre-cyclic and one-
directional. But more important is the fact that there are apparently
explanatory gaps and dilemmas inherent to ALL formulations of
pronominalization rules in ordered-base grammars. (See Bach
[1969] for arguments that the conventional Ross-Langacker type
of pronominalization cannot be a pre-cyclic, cyclic, or post-cyclic
rule without contradicting known facts and/or other conventional
assumptions and rules.) We will thus turn now to the much smoother
and straighter explanatory path that is opened up by the assumption of axiomatically unordered structures and derivational ordering rules.

An adequate treatment of anaphora formation in ordered base
and unordered base theories alike would have to take account of the
intimate relations between anaphora and destressing (see Gleitman
1965, Sanders 1967), as well as the relations between both anaphoric
and stress reductions and the general process of identity deletion
(see Sanders 1967). It appears thus far that the simplest and most
natural explanation of all anaphoric structures is by means of a
single cyclic or precedence-ordered deletion transformation which
effects the progressive redundancy-eliminating reduction of one of
two identical structures by the progressive deletion of the most
specific, or most deeply included, constituents of that structure.
This hypothesis is most strongly supported, perhaps, by the fact,
which has been observed by Lakoff (1968), that the relation between
possible anaphoric expressions and their possible antecedents is

HIERARCHIC — that is, for example, that a proper name (e.g. *Napoleon*) can be an antecedent to either an epithet (e.g. *that bastard*) or a pronoun (e.g. *he*), while an epithet can only be an antecedent to a pronoun and a pronoun cannot be an antecedent to anything. The particular hierarchy that Lakoff discusses (1. proper names, 2. definite descriptions, 3. epithets, 4. pronouns) would ultimately have to be reduced, of course, to a more general hierarchy which also accounts for the fact that stressed, indefinite, and restrictively relativized nominals can be antecedent to but not anaphoric to nominals which are respectively unstressed, definite, and lacking restrictive relativization. But regardless of the ultimate nature or complexity of this hierarchy it is clear that the fact that such hierarchical relations hold between antecedents and their anaphoric counterparts cannot possibly be EXPLAINED if the hierarchy itself is simply INCORPORATED into a grammar or theory of grammar as an *ad hoc* condition on the well-formedness of certain structures or on the application of certain grammatical rules. In other words these hierarchical relations can be explained only if they are NOT STIPULATED by any linguistic theory, but rather follow necessarily as logical CONSEQUENCES of general grammatical principles and initial conditions which make no reference whatever to the existence of the hierarchy or any particular members of it. At present the only principles which appear to be appropriate to this task are the principles of identity deletion and cyclic rule applicability and the only initial conditions which appear to be relevant are the groupings of specific, referential, and attributive constituents relative to each other and their generic heads.

The preceding remarks concern the CO-OCCURRENCE of antecedents and anaphoric reductions in utterances, and not the logically quite distinct matter of the RELATIVE ORDER of antecedents and their co-occurring reductions. These remarks thus apply to grammars which allow axiomatic ordering as well as to those that do not. We will thus assume that, regardless of differences in metatheoretical ordering constraints, all grammars will need to provide some explanation for progressive despeciations such as

(100) A boy who was *LAUGHING* came in, and [THAT,
SAME, MASCULINE, [ONE, [BOY, [WHO WAS
LAUGHING, [*STRESS*]]]]] sat down—deletion →
A boy *who was laughing* came in, and [THAT, SAME
MASCULINE, [ONE, [BOY, [*WHO WAS LAUGH-
ING*]]]] sat down—deletion →
A *boy* who was laughing came in, and [THAT, SAME,
MASCULINE, [ONE, [*BOY*]]] sat down—deletion →
A boy who was laughing came in, and [THAT, SAME,
MASCULINE, [*ONE*]] sat down—deletion →
A boy who was laughing came in, and [*THAT, SAME,
MASCULINE*] sat down—lexicalization →
A boy who was laughing came in and *he* sat down

The theory of anaphora-formation by progressive identity deletion would similarly apply, in ordered as well as unordered base
grammars, to account for the formation of epithets, such as
Lakoff's example (1968: 17, sentence (139)),

(101) Napoleon entered the room and that bastard announced
that Jean-Luc would hang,[6]

by principled derivations of the following sort:

[6] Lakoff's actual example, which is ungrammatical in my dialect, has *the* in
place of *that*. Since in my dialect *the* and *that* generally occur only in poly-
generic and monogeneric contexts, respectively,

(a) *A boy* and *a girl* came in, and *the boy* (*that boy) was smiling
(b) *A boy* came in, and *that boy* (*the boy) was smiling,

the acceptability of *that* rather than *the* in (101) is consistent with the proposed
hypothesis that epithets are derived from constructions whose heads are gener-
ically-identical to their antecedents in monogeneric domains of reference.
Compare, e.g.

(c) **A boy and an emperor came in, and the/that bastard announced that
Jean-Luc would hang.

There are many very interesting unsolved problems here, of course, and one
can do little more than speculate about them at this stage. One fact which
appears particularly relevant, though, is that when attributives occur with a
nominal epithet the acceptability of *the* as a possible substitute for *that* appears to increase with the number and/or length of the attributives; the following expansions of the epithet of (101) are thus increasingly acceptable:

(102)   Napoleon entered the room, that Napoleon announced
         that Jean-Luc would hang, that Napoleon is a bastard
         —subordination →
         Napoleon entered the room, and that Napoleon, *who is* a
         bastard, announced that Jean-Luc would hang—sub-
         ordinative reduction →
         Napoleon entered the room, and that *Napoleon*, a bastard,
         announced that Jean-Luc would hang—deletion →
         Napoleon entered the room and that *a* bastard announced
         that Jean-Luc would hang—unstressed indefinite sup-
         pression →
         Napoleon entered the room and that bastard announced
         that Jean-Luc would hang

In ordered-base grammars, however, it is obviously very difficult
to separate the treatment of anaphora-formation from the treatment of the order restrictions which hold between particular
antecedents and their particular anaphoric reductions. But the truly
critical problem for such grammars is raised by the fact that if
structures are axiomatically ordered anaphora formation MUST
be defined on ORDERED structures either before, after, or both
before and after certain RE-ORDERINGS of antecedents and their
reductions are effected. Since serious complications arise with
respect to each of these alternatives, though, and since these problems can apparently be solved only by the multiplication of *ad hoc*
restrictions on the relative ordering of particular rules which have
nothing whatever to do with anaphora, these grammars appear
to be inherently incapable of revealing the general PRINCIPLES
which are necessary and sufficient to account for the processes of
anaphoric reduction and ordering. It would seem evident, in fact,
that since it is neither necessary nor sufficient to know the RELATIVE

(d)   the bastard
(e)   the dirty bastard
(f)   the dirty low-down bastard.

None of these sound as good with *the* as with *that* though, no matter how long
and complex the epithet becomes.

ORDER of X and Y to know whether or not X is the antecedent of Y, the only reasonable and natural principles of anaphora-formation must be principles which apply with respect to UNORDERED structures. Similarly, since restrictions on the relative order of antecedents and their anaphoric reductions are restrictions on the ORDERING of constituents, it is only reasonable to suppose that they are most appropriately accounted for by rules that SPECIFY the correct ORDER of constituents in some or all languages.

For grammars which observe the Invariant Order Constraint on derivational ordering, the distinct processes of anaphora-formation and the ordering of anaphoric constituents relative to their antecedents can (and must) be specified by entirely distinct rules. It can readily be seen that the simplest and most general formulation of these rules requires that the order-independent process of anaphora-formation be specified with respect to unordered structures prior to the application of any ordering rules which effect or refer to the ordering of constituents including antecedents and their anaphoras; since anaphorically-related constituents are more restricted in their ordering than other constituents, it is also clear that any ordering rules which make special reference to anaphoric constituents must be assumed to apply prior to the application of the more general ordering rules for clause-constituents (93) and the most general rule for free, or commutative, ordering: $[X, Y] \rightarrow [X \& Y]$.

We will assume then that anaphora-formation in all languages is specified by a cyclic identity deletion transformation that is defined on unordered structures in which the attributes of all nominals are hierarchically grouped with STRESS as the most deeply included constituent and with the maximally generic features of the nominal (e.g. NOMINAL, ANIMATE, HUMAN, referential marking, etc.) as its least included (immediate) constituents. This rule might be formulated in some such way as the following:

(103) ANAPHORA-FORMATION

$$\frac{[W, [N, x, [Y, [Z]]]], [U, [N, x, [Y, [Z]]]]}{1 \qquad\qquad\qquad\qquad 2} \rightarrow 1 \ \emptyset$$

We will assume for present purposes that this rule applies obligatorily on its first cycle and optionally elsewhere; such applicability may or may not be a general property of grammatical rules of this type, but in any event it is necessary to assure that, except where contrastive stressing applies, all but one of any set of referentially-identical nominals in any discourse must be destressed.[7] This rule has also been arbitrarily restricted so as to effect reductions only of nominal phrases and sentences, since these are the only types of constituents which have the generic property N(ominal); if there are any other types of constituents, and if they undergo parallel reductions, the rule could easily be generalized to accomodate these. It will also be observed, of course, that the processes of Coordinative Reduction and Anaphora Formation are intimately related, and that the former might be viewed as nothing more than an extension of the latter process of progressive deletion from identical species to identical genera. For present purposes, however, it makes no difference whether these are reduced to a single rule or not.

After the application of Anaphora Formation and all other non-ordering, non-lexical, and non-phonological rules of the grammar EVERY PAIR of nominal structures included in any linguistic representation will be FORMALLY CHARACTERIZED as either (a) NON-ANAPHORIC, (b) EQUALLY ANAPHORIC, or (c) DIFFERENTIALLY ANAPHORIC:

(104)   (a)   NON-ANAPHORIC:
        ... [N, x, [Y]] ... [N, -x, [Z]] ...

---

[7] Elsewhere (Sanders 1967: sec. 5.2) I have formulated Contrastive Stressing as a rule which adds STRESS to the non-identical constituents of partially-identical sentences. In this framework it would be possible to account for the absence of stress on the members of anaphoric sets simply as a consequence of the non-applicability of the Contrastive Stressing rule to such constituents. However, it might also be possible to account for all occurrences of contrastive stress simply as a consequence of the non-applicability of Anaphora-Formation to non-identical constituents. At present, I know of no convincing reasons for preferring either of these alternatives to the other, or even for assuming that contrastive stressing and destressing are necessarily only two sides of the same coin.

(b) EQUALLY-ANAPHORIC:
... $[N, x, [Y]]$ ... $[N, x, [Y]]$ ...

(c) DIFFERENTIALLY-ANAPHORIC:

$$\underbrace{... [N, x, [Y, [Z]]]}_{more\ antecedent} \underbrace{... [N, x, [Y]]}_{more\ anaphoric^8} ... \quad [Z \neq null]$$

There are, of course, no restrictions on the relative ordering of specifically-distinct non-anaphoric constituents or equally-anaphoric constituents:

(105) (a) Peter saw a *raccoon*, and Jane saw an *armadillo*
             Jane saw an *armadillo*, and Peter saw a *raccoon*
       (b) Peter saw a raccoon; *it* was eating, and *it* was drinking
             Peter saw a raccoon; *it* was drinking, and *it* was eating

The only problem of anaphoric ordering is thus the problem of specifying the proper relative order of differentially-anaphoric constituents:

(106) Jane saw *an armadillo*, and *that armadillo* was sleeping
       *That armadillo was sleeping, and Jane saw *an armadillo*

It is appropriate to begin with the clearest and most transparently-explainable instances of correct and incorrect ordering of these differentially-anaphoric constituents, namely instances involving the ordering of obviously coordinate structures, as in (106) or (107).

(107) (a) *Napoleon* was born in Corsica, and *he* was crowned in Paris
             *He was crowned in Paris, and *Napoleon* was born in Corsica

---

[8] For any arbitrarily-large set of differentially-anaphoric constituents, then, there is an effective procedure for specifying a unique partial-order ranking of its members from the most antecedent to the least antecedent, or, inversely, from the most anaphoric to the least anaphoric. This procedure depends solely on the formal properties of unordered non-phonological representations of linguistic objects subsequent to the application of Anaphora Formation.

In connection with the notation for generic non-identity in (104a), it should be recalled that lower case variables stand for sets of single generic (immediate) constituents of constructions, and that the notation -A stands for any set of structures that are not analyzable as A.

(b) I met *a girl* yesterday; *the girl that I met* was wearing
a green hat, and everyone was looking at *her*

**The girl that I met* was wearing a green hat; I met
a girl yesterday, and everyone was looking at *her*

*I met *her* yesterday; everyone was looking at *a girl*,
and *the girl that I met* was wearing a green hat

(c) *That cat on the mat* is mine; *that cat*'s dreaming of
rats

*That cat's dreaming of rats; *that cat on the mat* is
mine

(d) *Lucifer* and the girl who *he* was dancing with were
laughing

*The girl who *he* was dancing with and *Lucifer* were
laughing

(e) Do *lemurs* sleep at night or during the day? *They*
sleep during the day

*They sleep during the day. Do *lemurs* sleep at night
or during the day?

*Do *they* sleep at night or during the day? *Lemurs*
sleep during the day.

The governing principle here, of course, is that antecedents
precede their anaphoric reductions, or, more precisely, that for
any differentially-anaphoric pair of nominals the constituent
which includes the more antecedent member of the pair must be
ordered before the sister constituent which includes the more
anaphoric member. This principle can be expressed by a general
Anaphoric Ordering rule, which could be formulated as (108).

(108) ANAPHORIC ORDERING

$$\frac{[[W,[N, x, [Y,[Z]]]], [U, [N, x, [Y]]]]}{1 \qquad\qquad\qquad 2} \rightarrow 1\ \&\ 2$$

Like all rules employing unrestricted variables, this rule subsumes
an infinite number of sub-rules, which, according to a generally-
accepted convention (see Chomsky 1967), are sequentially ordered
in such a way that sub-rules with longer strings as values for the

variables are applicable before or instead of all sub-rules with shorter strings as their values. Given this convention the Anaphoric Ordering rule will correctly effect the ordering of any arbitrary number of differentially-anaphoric constituents in any arbitrarily long representation by first ordering the constituent including the most antecedent nominal in the representation (i.e. the nominal with the longest analyses as Y and Z) before the sister constituent with the next most antecedent nominal (i.e. the one with the longest analysis as Y), then ordering the second most antecedent constituent before the third most antecedent one, etc.

There is a very interesting relationship between this principle of Anaphoric Ordering and the principle which governs the relative order of sister constituents which include nominals which are non-identical in reference but identical in all other axiomatic properties. From the more obvious examples involving the order of numerated and overtly-referenced constituents, as in (109-111),

(109)   I saw one two three four five sparrows
        *I saw four one three five two sparrows
(110)   I saw one sparrow and another sparrow
        *I saw another sparrow and one sparrow
(111)   A boy was laughing, and a second boy was crying
        *A second boy was crying, and a boy was laughing,

it is evident that the basic principle here is essentially the reverse of that which governs the ordering of ordinary referentially-identical anaphoric constituents; thus where species are identical and genera differ with respect to otherness marking (see Sanders 1967: Sec. 4.7), constituents with LONGER GENERA are ordered AFTER co-specific constituents with SHORTER GENERA, e.g.

(112)   (a)   [ONE] & [ONE, ONE] & [ONE, ONE, ONE] & ...
        (b)   [[ONE, MASCULINE, HUMAN, [BOY]], WAS
              LAUGHING] & [[ONE, OTHER, MASCULINE,
              HUMAN, [BOY]], WAS CRYING],

while for ordinary anaphoric ordering, where species are different and genera identical, constituents with LONGER SPECIES are ordered

BEFORE co-generic constituents with SHORTER SPECIES. In other words, we really have a single complementary principle here governing the relative ordering of related nominals:

(113)   For any two nominals N_1 analyzable as $[N, X, Y]$ and N_2 analyzable as $[N, X]$, if Y is a most included specific constituent, N_1 is ordered before N_2, and if Y is a referential (otherness) constituent, N_2 is ordered before N_1.

If we assume an abbreviatory convention for disjunctive conflation whereby any statement of the form (a) is an abbreviation for the (simultaneously-ordered) statements (b) and (c),

(114)   (a)   ... (A/B) ... (C/D) ...
         (b)   ... (A)   ... (C) ...
         (c)   ...   (B)   ... (D) ...,

we can formulate the general rule for related nominal ordering as a single conflation of some such form as the following:

(115)   RELATED NOMINAL ORDERING
$$\underline{[W, [N, x, (\emptyset/\text{OTHER}), [Y, (Z/\emptyset)]]]}, \underline{[U, [N, x, [Y]]]}$$
$$\quad\quad\quad\quad 1 \quad\quad\quad\quad\quad\quad\quad\quad\quad 2 \;\to (1 \,\&\, 2/2 \,\&\, 1)$$

The simultaneity, or mutual non-precedence of the two ordering processes conflated here is crucial, since any structure which satisfies BOTH the conditions for differential species ordering AND the conditions for differential otherness ordering must also satisfy BOTH product descriptions of the subrules of (115), one with respect to the ordering of its antecedents relative to their reductions, the other with respect to the relative ordering of its referentially-distinct co-specific constituents.

Thus, for any structures which satisfy the structural descriptions of BOTH subrules of (115), such as the structures underlying (116a-d), the structure resulting from the application of one of the subrules must be IDENTICAL to that resulting from the application of the other subrule, as is the case for (116a), since ungrammaticality follows not only from the failure to satisfy ANY of the product

descriptions of the rule, as in (116b), but also from the failure to satisfy ALL of its product descriptions, as in (116c) and 116d):

(116) (a) *A dog* was chasing *John*, and *another dog* was barking at *him*
       (b) **Another dog* was barking at *him*, and *a dog* was chasing *John*
       (c) **A dog* was chasing *him*, and *another dog* was barking at *John*
       (d) **Another dog* was chasing *John*, and *a dog* was barking at *him*

The fact that there are structures such as (116c-d) which have *no* correct ordering is accounted for by the fact that, although Related Nominal Ordering is OBLIGATORY and although these structures satisfy its structural descriptions, the rule CANNOT apply to these structures in any way which will not violate at least one of its sub-rules. This is the standard metatheoretical characterization of an intrinsically and irremediably ill-formed derivation — a derivation which includes a line which both must and must not undergo some obligatory transformation. Thus if the condition of product-description compatibility is a general condition on the application of all obligatory transformations, then the general Related Nominal Ordering rule (115) will correctly effect the appropriate ordering of all derivationally well-formed coordinative structures including related nominals and will properly "block" on all structures which are irremediably ill-formed with respect to their potentiality for grammatically-correct ordering of their constituents.

If this general sub-rule compatibility condition should prove to be empirically indefensible, however, it would then presumably be necessary either to greatly complicate the specification of anaphora formation and referencing or to abandon the specification of ordering by means of possibly sequential transformational rules in favor of a system of simultaneously applicable well-formedness conditions on randomly-ordered surface structures, or a system of unordered "anywhere" conditions, or "redundancy rules", making use of one or more ordering features with the contradiction of

feature values as the formal characterization of irremediable un-grammaticality. Both of these latter alternatives appear to be excessively powerful in some respects, and at the same time inherently incapable of explaining or revealing some things which are readily accounted for by means of the metatheoretically more-restricted alternative of transformational ordering rules. Thus, for example, it would appear that neither well-formedness conditions nor ordering feature predictions would be capable of formally differentiating a sentence such as (116b), which is incorrectly ordered but COULD have been correctly ordered, from sentences such as (116c-d), which have NO POSSIBLE correct orderings. Given the compatibility of products condition, on the other hand, and the metatheoretical requirement of transformational ordering, the latter cases of inherent ungrammaticality are differentiated from the former case of accidental or remediable deviance by the fact that in the former case there is no incompatibility of product descriptions while in the latter there is. Pending further study, then, we will assume that the compatibility of products condition is correct for obligatory rules and that ordering is most appropriately specified by rules rather than conditions.[9]

---

[9]   The same argument applies to Perlmutter's output-condition treatment of clitic pronoun ordering in Spanish (Perlmutter 1968: Chapter 4), since such a treatment is incapable of differentiating cases of remediably incorrect ordering, such as (a), from cases of irremediable ungrammaticality such as (b):

   (a) *le me escapé (cf. me le escapé, 'I escaped from him')
   (b) *te me escapé (cf. *me te escapé, where *me* is reflexive)

However, given a precedence-relational ordering rule of the form

   (c)   SPANISH CLITIC ORDERING

$$[[\text{CLITIC.} \begin{Bmatrix} \text{[REFLEXIVE]} \\ \text{[2nd PERSON]} \\ \text{[1st PERSON]} \\ \text{[3rd PERSON]} \end{Bmatrix}], [\text{VERB}], X]$$

   $\underline{12\rightarrow 1\ \&\ 2,}$

sentences such as *me le escapé* and *le me escapé* would be derivable by the proper and improper application of rule (c), respectively, while the structure underlying sentences such as *te me escapé* and *me te escapé*, in consequence of the Compatibility of Products Condition, will have NO POSSIBLE correct product of the rule. See also Note 11 of Chapter 2, and Sanders (1970).

The preceding remarks are of some importance for the substantiation of invariant derivational ordering, and they have a direct bearing on the important task of determining the proper form and function of ordering specifications. They are not directly relevant to the problem of accounting for Postal's crossover phenomena, however, since these particular phenomena appear to be restricted to violability with respect to non-coordinate differentially anaphoric constituents alone. We will return now to this central problem, and to the specification of anaphoric ordering with respect to constituents which are not obviously coordinative.

The basic anaphoric restrictions with respect to clearly subordinative constructions are illustrated by sentence-sets such as the following (Lakoff 1968: 2):

(117) (a) *John* ate supper before *he* left town
      (b) **He* ate supper before *John* left town
      (c) Before *John* left town, *he* ate supper
      (d) Before *he* left town, *John* ate supper

(118) (a) *John* saw a snake near *him*
      (b) **He* saw a snake near *John*
      (c) *Near *John,* *he* saw a snake
      (d) Near *him,* *John* saw a snake

There are, of course, many other types of data which would have to be taken into account by any fully adequate treatment of anaphoric ordering in subordinative constructions; for present purposes, however, we will ignore other factors and will consider these particular data as representative of the major explanatory problems involved. Sentences such as (117) show that, when one differentially anaphoric constituent is in a superordinate clause and the other is in a clause subordinate to it, a subordinate antecedent must always precede a superordinate anaphora, while a superordinate antecedent may either precede or follow a subordinate anaphora. Sentences such as (118), on the other hand, reveal a restriction of a quite different sort, namely that it can never be the case that an antecedent is included in a PHRASE which is subordinate to a constituent which includes its anaphoric reduction. It can

readily be seen that the latter restriction is directly relevant to the problem of crossover phenomena, and that, unlike the former, it is not an ordering restriction at all, but rather a restriction either on anaphora FORMATION or on the REDUCTION of subordinate clauses including anaphoric constituents. We will thus wish to focus our attention here on the problem of anaphoric relations between superordinate and subordinate phrases.

First, however, it will be useful to have a general representation of the data illustrated by (117) and (118) which will reveal the grouping relations between each antecedent and anaphora. Assuming the previously-discussed convention for the preservation and elimination of bracketing, and assuming also that phrases like *near him* in (118) are the products of derivational reductions applied to structures underlying complete clauses like *which was near him* and *that snake was near him*, we might represent the general structures instanced by (117) and (118) in the following variable-suppressed form:

(119) (a) $_s$[ANTECEDENT $_s$[ANAPHORA]]
             (d) $_s$[$_s$[ANAPHORA] ANTECEDENT]
       (b) *$_s$[ANAPHORA $_s$[ANTECEDENT]]
             (c) $_s$[$_s$[ANTECEDENT] ANAPHORA]
(120) (a) [ANTECEDENT [ANAPHORA]]
             (d) [[ANAPHORA] ANTECEDENT]
       (b) *[ANAPHORA [ANTECEDENT]]
             (c) *[[ANTECEDENT] ANAPHORA]

It can be seen from this display that except for (119c) all well-formed differentially anaphoric constructions have antecedents which are not subordinate to their anaphoric reductions. (This is of course also true for coordinative configurations, in which neither the antecedent nor the anaphoric constituent is subordinate to the other.) If we could account in some way for the peculiarity of (119c) in this respect, then, all of the other relevant facts could be accounted for by a revision of the Anaphora Formation rule (103) in such a way that constituents are deletable only in relation to identical constituents which are coordinate or superordinate to

them. This appears to be a reasonable and perhaps independently motivated restriction, possibly even one which follows from entirely independent metatheoretical constraints on the analysis of all grammatical statements. However, since I know of no sufficiently well-motivated way of accounting for the exceptionality of (119c) with respect to the principle of non-subordinate antecedence, the tasks of explaining the subordinative clause data of (119) will be left uncompleted here. It should be noted, though, that even in the case of the clause data, the fundamental problem here is NOT one of ORDERING, since the commutativity of the subordinate and superordinate constituents of (119a-d), like that of (120a-d), follows quite regularly from the fact that these structures do not satisfy the general conditions for (coordinative) Anaphoric or Related Nominal Ordering and thus will presumably remain un-ordered, along with various non-anaphoric subordinative and coordinative structures, until the final, or "elsewhere", Commutative Ordering rule is applicable. The most significant generalization here, in fact, appears to be precisely that there are NO ordering restrictions between a superordinate antecedent and its subordinate reduction.

Regardless of how the clause data of (119) are ultimately accounted for, though, there would appear to be only two possible ways of explaining the phrasal anaphoric restrictions of (120): (1) by preventing the desentential reduction of antecedent clauses such as (119b-c) to antecedent phrases such as (120b-c), or (2) by preventing Anaphora Formation from applying in such a way as to effect the deletion of any superordinate phrasal constituent in terms of any phrasal constituent that is subordinate to it. Although the first alternative cannot be excluded on any *a priori* grounds of inherent implausibility or unnaturalness, we will assume here that the second alternative is fundamentally correct and will restrict our attention to it alone.

The Anaphora Formation rule formulated previously (103) applies only with respect to pairs of sister constituents where neither of the nominals included in these constituents is subordinate to the other. This restriction is determined in part by a fairly common

particular convention associated with the analysis of free variables, or cover symbols: namely, that no cover symbol may include an unclosed parenthesization. If we replace this convention with another one, however, we find that the proper extension of the applicability of Anaphora Formation will be expressed by a rule which is substantively simpler than the original coordinatively-restricted one or any similarly restricted rule in accordance with the new convention for variable-analysis.

Let us tentatively accept, then, the universal analysis convention

(121)   For any grammatical rule or metarule which refers to any structure *AXB*, where *X* is one of the set of free variables, or cover symbols, specified by the governing metatheory, and for any linguistic representation *S*, *AXB* refers to *S* if and only if *S* is analyzable as *ACB*, where *C* is free of unclosed right brackets.

In terms of this convention, in other words, a representation such as (122a) could refer to representations such as (122b-e), but not to any of the representations illustrated by (122f-h):

(122)   (a)   [NOMINAL], X, [NOMINAL]
        (b)   [NOMINAL], [A, B, C, D], [NOMINAL]
        (c)   [NOMINAL], [A, [B, C], D], [NOMINAL]
        (d)   [NOMINAL], [A, B, C, D, [NOMINAL]
        (e)   [NOMINAL], A, B, [C, [D, [NOMINAL
        (f)   *[NOMINAL], A, B,], C], D, [NOMINAL]
        (g)   *[NOMINAL], A, [B, C], D], [NOMINAL]
        (h)   *[NOMINAL], A], B], [C, D, [NOMINAL]

The choice of excluding unclosed right brackets rather than un-closed left brackets is of course entirely arbitrary here, though if there are any syntactic or phonological rules which apply to ordered structures or conflate ordering with extraposition, some motivations might be found for the general characterization of A rather than B as the necessarily non-subordinated member of any AXB configuration. In any event this convention makes the empirically-testable claim that there are many significant grammatical rules

which apply with respect to some constituents A and B BOTH when A and B are coordinate AND when ONE of the constituents is subordinate to the other (say B to A), but do NOT apply if the subordination relation is reversed (i.e. if A is subordinate to B). (See Ross [1967], Postal [1971] for extensive discussion of various related claims about bounding and variable analysis.)

If this convention proves to be empirically defensible, the Anaphora Formation rule (103) for coordinative structures could be replaced by the more general rule (123), which will also effect the correct anaphoric reductions in subordinative structures:

(123) ANAPHORA-FORMATION (Coordinative and Subordinative)
$$\underline{[N, x, [Y, [Z]]], W, [N, x, [Y, [Z]]]}_{1\qquad\qquad\qquad\qquad 2} \rightarrow 1\ \emptyset$$

If the convention is not defensible, separate rules for coordinative and subordinative Anaphora Formation would be required, although some other more complex form of conflation might also be possible.

We are now ready to return to the active-passive alternation in English and the precise nature of the restriction underlying the contrasting grammaticality of sentences like (124a) and (124b-d).

(124) (a) Lucifer scratched himself
       (b) *He/himself scratched Lucifer
       (c) *He/himself was scratched by Lucifer
       (d) *Lucifer was scratched by himself,

Though (d) is of course only mildly deviant with respect to the grossly ungrammatical pronominal-subject sentences (b) and (c), it is clearly quite deviant with respect to such fully normal sentences as

(125) (a) Lucifer was scratched by Gabriel
       (b) *Gabriel* may have been scratched by somebody *else*, but *Lucifer* was scratched by *himself*.

For present purposes, in any event, we will follow Postal in taking the grammaticality specifications of (124) as given.

The superficial structures of active and passive sentences prior to the application of the Nominal Ordering rule (93) have been assumed to be

(126) (a) [[AGENT], [[-AGENT], [VERB]]]
       (b) [[-AGENT], [[AGENT], [VERB]]],

where the passive structure (126b) is assumed to be optionally derived from some derivationally prior active structure of the form (126a). Let us assume for the present that this derivation is effected by an optional regrouping transformation which has (126a) as its input description and (126b) as its output description; let us call this transformation Passive Formation. It is clear, of course, that Passive Formation can only apply before Nominal Ordering, since the former rule is defined on unordered configurations which are eliminated by the application of the latter rule. This metatheoretically-determined ordering is also the only empirically-defensible ordering of these rules, since there would be no other way to express the significant generalization that in English ALL superficial subjects are ordered pre-verbally and ALL superficial complements post-verbally regardless of their non-superficial properties and groupings.

Considering now the case where the Agent and non Agent of a transitive structure like (126a) are identical, we must determine the applicability relations between the processes of Anaphora Formation and Anaphoric Ordering and the general rules of Passive Formation and Nominal Ordering. If Anaphora Formation were to apply after Passive Formation, then it would apply to both (126a) and (126b) to yield (127a) and (127b), respectively.

(127) (a) [[AGENT, ANTECEDENT], [[-AGENT, ANAPHORA], [VERB]]]
       (b) [[-AGENT, ANTECEDENT], [[AGENT, ANAPHORA], [VERB]]].

Nominal Ordering would then apply to these structures to yield sentences such as (124a) and (124d), respectively. While this treatment would thus account for the ungrammaticality of all active and passive sentences with anaphoric subjects and antecedent non-

subjects (124 b, c), it fails to account for the ungrammaticality of sentences with destressed anaphoric agent complements (124d) relative to normal sentences with anaphoric patient complements (124a). The treatment fails, in other words, to account for the apparent crossover restriction on alternations of the active-passive type. To eliminate this inadequacy it would be necessary to impose some restriction on Passive Formation which would effectively prevent its application to structures with identical Agents and non-Agents. Since non-Agents would thus always remain subordinate to their identical Agents, Anaphora Formation would always effect the reduction of the non-Agent in any such structure. Thus with the application of Nominal Ordering, sentences such as (124a) would be derived and all of the non-grammatical sentences (124 b-d) would be underivable.

The required restriction could be effected by means of a simple constraint against the regrouping of referentially identical nominals relative to each other:

(128)   CO-REFERENTIAL NON-ASSOCIATIVITY CONSTRAINT: For any linguistic derivation D and any line X included in D, if X is analyzable as [A [[N, W, [CASE, Z]], [N, W, [CASE, -Z]], Y]] B], then there is no line X' included in D such that X' is analyzable as [A [[N, W, [CASE, -Z]], [[N, W, [CASE, Z], Y]] B]; i.e. the relative grouping of co-referential nominals of non-identical case is derivationally invariant.

This constraint is neither more nor less *ad hoc* than Postal's Crossover Principle, and since it effects exactly the same filtering function as the latter while being fully compatible with the Invariant Order Constraint, it follows that the Invariant Order Constraint cannot be empirically falsified with respect to any facts about crossover phenomena of the active-passive type.[10]

---

[10] It should be noted in particular that this invariant derivational ordering treatment is equivalent to Postal's axiomatic variable ordering treatment even with respect to the proper ranking of the more (124 b,c) and less (124 d) ungrammatical members of sets such as (124). Thus, for Postal, the difference

Postal says nothing about the naturalness or plausibility of his Crossover Principle, or about its possible reduction to any principles of a more general character. Although it is clear that the proposed constraint against coreferential regrouping is certainly no less natural or plausible than Postal's constraint against coreferential reordering, I am unable here to provide any convincing explanation of non-associativity in terms of any more general principles of grammar. What has been shown then is that there is an equally adequate — and not necessarily superior — account of active-passive type crossover phenomena which requires no reordering rules, and thus that grammars which observe the Invariant Order Constraint are sufficient — but not necessarily necessary — for the principled explanation of such phenomena. Although this demonstration suffices for present purposes, we will conclude now with some remarks on the possible directions which might be taken

---

here is accounted for by the fact that (124d) is derivable only by violating the Crossover Principle, while (124b) violates the conditions for pronominalization and/or reflexivization, and (124c) apparently violates both these conditions and the Crossover Constraint. One might expect from this characterization, however, that (124b) should be somehow less deviant than (124c), although, for my dialect at least, these appear to be equally bad, or, if anything, (124b) seems a little MORE deviant than (124c). In the alternative treatment proposed here, (124d) violates only the Coreferential Non-Associativity Constraint; (124b) and (124c) violate both Anaphora Formation and Anaphoric Ordering, and (124c) also violates the Non-Associativity Constraint. Thus both treatments explain why sentences like (124d) are more ungrammatical than sentences like (124b), and both fail to explain why (124b) is equal or greater in deviance than (124c); only the derivational ordering treatment, though, offers an explanation for the greater deviance of (124c) relative to (124d), since this treatment allows for the derivation of the former only if three conditions are violated, while the latter is derivable if only one condition is violated.

It should also be noted that the problem of "keeping track" of initial structural relations, which plagues any attempted formulation of the crossover principle as a derivational constraint on reordering, does not arise with respect to the Coreferential Non-Associativity Constraint. This is because this constraint makes use only of the INDEPENDENTLY-MOTIVATED inherent case and otherness properties of nominals in determining whether a nominal in one line of a derivation is or is not the same nominal as that occurring in another line. It is thus not necessary to know anything about that INITIAL grouping of structures in order to correctly apply the Non-Associativity Constraint, nothing more being required than a pairwise comparison of the independently motivated representations constituting the lines of any derivation.

in attempting to explain the non-associativity constraint. These remarks will also serve to illustrate its effectiveness with respect to the characterization of complement alternations and other facts subsumed by the notion of crossover phenomena.

The restriction that is required to prevent Passive Formation from applying in the case of identical nominals obviously cannot be expressed by a particular condition on this particular rule — first, because such rule-specific conditions are properly excluded by adequate explanatory theories of grammar, but, more importantly, because restrictions precisely parallel to this one would clearly be required with respect to the application of other transformations which either are or are not conflatable with Passive Formation. Thus we would expect that whatever condition prevents the application of Passive Formation to identical nominals will also effectively prevent under the same conditions the application of whatever rule underlies such complement alternations as

(129) (a) Elizabeth talked to Lucifer about Gabriel
       (b) Elizabeth talked about Gabriel to Lucifer
       (c) Elizabeth talked to Lucifer about himself
       (d) *Elizabeth talked about Lucifer to him(self).

Passive Formation is a conflation of two elementary regrouping, or association, transformations; we will assume here, without giving motivations for the assumption, that of these two elementary subrules, Complement Raising (i) is formulated so as to feed Agent Lowering (ii), although the relative order of application of the two intrinsically related processes is arbitrary and irrelevant with respect to the present discussion:

(130) (i)   [[AGENT], [[-AGENT], X]] → [[AGENT],
             [-AGENT], [X]]
       (ii) [[-AGENT], [AGENT], [X]] → [[-AGENT],
             [[AGENT], X]]

We will also assume that complement alternations are effected by similar regrouping transformations. To account for the Dative and non-Dative alternations in sentences such as (131), let us as-

sume tentatively and without sufficient justification that a sentence such as (a) is derived from a structure such as (b), which might be roughly "translated" as (c):

(131) (a) Elizabeth talked to Lucifer about Gabriel
       (b) [[AGENT, ELIZABETH], [[DATIVE, LUCIFER], [[-DATIVE, GABRIEL] [TALK]]]]
       (c) Elizabeth was the agent of Lucifer's being the recipient of Gabriel's being the topic of some talk-(ing)[11]

The Dative could, of course, be raised here and the Agent lowered by Passive Formation, yielding

(132) (a) Lucifer was talked to by Elizabeth about Gabriel
       (b) Lucifer was talked to about Gabriel by Elizabeth.

We observe, moreover, that the non-Dative can also be raised to the function of superficial subject:

(133) (a) Gabriel was talked about to Lucifer by Elizabeth
       (b) Gabriel was talked about by Elizabeth to Lucifer.

Since non-Agents can be interchanged with superordinate Agents, and non-Datives with superordinate Datives, it would thus not be unreasonable to assume that complement alternations and active-passive alternations may actually be subsumed by the same general process of nominal regrouping.

Thus Passive Formation, Non-Dative Raising, and other similar nominal regroupings might possibly all be reducible to a single

---

[11] There are many arguments which could be given in support of this line of derivation. For present purposes, however, it will suffice to merely note that (131c) is the ONLY MEANINGFUL hierarchical configuration of its constituent predications, all other logically-possible configurations being not only un-grammatical but also semantically ill-formed:

   (i) *Lucifer was the recipient of Elizabeth's being the agent of Gabriel's being the topic of some talk(ing)
  (ii) *Gabriel was the topic of Elizabeth's being the agent of Lucifer's being the recipient of some talk(ing)
 (iii) *Elizabeth was the agent of Gabriel's being the topic of Lucifer's being the recipient of some talk(ing)

more general rule of NOMINAL RAISING, a rule which might perhaps
be formulated as

(134)
[[N, W, [CASE, Z]], [[N, Y, [CASE, -Z]], X]]]
[1   [2   3]] → [2 [1 3]]

The Coreferential Non-Associativity Constraint would prevent the
application of this rule to any structures whose analyzed first
and second terms are coreferential, that is, any structure with
respect to which the strings W and Y are identical in its analysis as
(134). It would thus be possible to eliminate the Non-Associativity
Constraint by simply substituting -W for Y in the structural description of Nominal Raising (134); this would amount to the claim
that crossover deviance results not from the violation of any
metatheoretical constraint on analysis or derivation, but rather
simply from the application of a particular universal rule to structures which do not satisfy its structural description. The effectiveness of this treatment would depend, of course, on the reducib-
ility to Nominal Raising of a number of regrouping processes
which have thus far been treated by means of entirely distinct rules;
in addition to active-passive and dative-nondative alternations,
the general rule of Nominal Raising would also have to subsume
such alternations as those labeled by Postal (1971) as products of
"Tough Movement" (e.g. 135a) and "Psych Movement" (e.g.
135b):

(135)   (a)   It was difficult for Tony to hit Jack
              Jack was difficult for Tony to hit
              It was difficult for Tony to hit himself
              *Tony was difficult for him(self) to hit
              *He/himself was difficult for Tony to hit
        (b)   Lucifer accepts Gabriel
              Gabriel is acceptable to Lucifer
              Lucifer accepts himself
              *Lucifer is acceptable to him(self)
              *He/himself is acceptable to Lucifer

Since these and other crossover alternations are superficially quite similar to alternations of the active-passive and dative-nondative type, and particularly since all of these alternations clearly seem to involve at least one derivational regrouping of a pair of nominal constituents, the hypothesis that a single general rule of Nominal Raising is involved in the derivation of all sentences subject to crossover-type deviance would appear to be entirely plausible. The ultimate correctness of this hypothesis must of course be left as an open question here, however, and so too then the ultimate correctness of this possible reduction of the Non-Associativity Constraint.

It is also possible, of course, that all of these nominal alternations may ultimately be accounted for by a single process of nominal extraposition rather than regrouping, where, for example, from an axiomatically-undifferentiated structure such as (136a), the application of Nominal Extraposition (b) would effect such alternate groupings as (c-e):

(136) (a) [[AGENT], [DATIVE], [PATIENT], [VERB]]
       (b) [[NOMINAL], [VERB], X] → [[NOMINAL]
            [[VERB] X]]
       (c) [[AGENT], [[DATIVE], [[PATIENT], [[VERB]]]]]
       (d) [[DATIVE], [[AGENT], [[PATIENT], [[VERB]]]]]
       (e) [[PATIENT], [[DATIVE], [[AGENT], [[VERB]]]]]

There are certain precedence relations which must be observed, however, with respect to either Nominal Regrouping or Nominal Extraposition. Thus, for example, an Instrumental (or Inanimate Agent) can never be interchanged with or extraposed prior to an Agent (or Animate Instrument):

(137) (a) This door can be opened with a golden key
       (b) A golden key can open this door
       (c) This door can be opened with a golden key by the king
       (d) This door can be opened by the king with a golden key

   (e)   The king can open this door with a golden key

   (f)   *A golden key can open this door with/by the king

A similar precedence relation apparently holds between Manner and Reason nominals, a Manner expression never occurring super-ordinate to an associated Reason:

(138) (a)   Cleopatra ate the bananas greedily

       (b)   Greedily, Cleopatra ate the bananas

       (c)   Cleopatra ate the bananas greedily because she was hungry

       (d)   Because she was hungry, Cleopatra ate the bananas greedily

       (e)   *Greedily, Cleopatra ate the bananas because she was hungry

Reason expressions also take precedence over Instrumentals:

(139) (a)   Cleopatra peeled the bananas with her fingers be-cause she was hungry

       (b)   Because she was hungry, Cleopatra peeled the bananas with her fingers

(140) (a)   *Cleopatra peeled the bananas because she was hungry with her fingers

       (b)   *With her fingers, Cleopatra peeled the bananas be-cause she was hungry

However these various precedence relations are ultimately ac-counted for, it is evident that the non-associativity of coreferential nominals might be accounted for in the same way, since coreferential Agents, Datives, and non-Datives, for example, form a precedence hierarchy in the same sense as that formed by reference-irrelevant Agents, Instruments, and Reasons. Thus if the precedence hierarchy for nominal grouping relations were to be specified axiomatically or by well-formedness conditions on underlying and derived structures, the explanatory functions of Postal's Crossover Prin-ciple or the alternative Coreferential Non-Associativity Con-

straint (128) could also be achieved by the following general Hierarchical Grouping Constraint:

(141)   HIERARCHICAL GROUPING CONSTRAINT: For any specified partially-ordered precedence hierarchy (1 ... m ... n ...), where *m* (for example, Agent) is precedent to *n* (for example, coreferential non-Agent), *X* is a possible line in a derivation of some linguistic object only if *X* does not include any substring analyzable as [... [n, W, [[m, Y]]] ...], i.e. only if *n* is never superordinate to *m* in *X*.

It is evident, however, that the postulation of a precedence hierarchy does not really explain anything, since what we are actually most interested in explaining is indeed the hierarchy itself. Thus whether the hierarchy is one involving the relative initial order and possible reordering of differently-cased nominals as in Postal's treatment, or one involving the relative grouping of differently-cased nominals as in the alternative treatment proposed here, what we ultimately want to know is WHY certain structures take precedence over certain others with respect to the application of certain particular grammatical processes. Thus regardless of whether the principle of coreferential non-associativity is reduced to a more general principle of precedence-related grouping or not, we want to know WHAT essential properties of coreferential differently-cased nominals DETERMINE their apparent non-associativity and their particular positions in the general network of nominal grouping and ordering relations. These are several possible lines of investigation which might lead towards such an explanation, but at this stage it is not yet possible to determine which will ultimately prove to be the most rewarding. I will merely mention one of these here.

In brief, this approach would investigate the possibility of explaining nominal grouping relations in a manner precisely parallel to the manner in which the Related Nominal Ordering rule (115) explains the ordering relations between nominals in terms of the identity and non-identity of their generic and specific properties. Rule (115), it will be recalled, specifies that the referen-

tially shorter of two specifically-identical nominals is ordered first
and that the specifically-shorter of two referentially-identical
nominals is ordered last. Now let us assume, contrary to our previous assumptions, that there is no rule of Nominal Raising and
that all superficial groupings are derived by Nominal Extraposition
(as in (136)) from axiomatic constructions consisting of a predicative constituent and a set of nominals as immediate constituents.
As noted previously, such an extraposition rule might be formulated
possibly as

(142)   [[NOMINAL], [VERB], X] → [[NOMINAL],
        [[VERB], X]]

Let us also tentatively assume now that Anaphora Formation can
apply BEFORE the application of this extraposition rule, and let us
consider how the anaphoric precedence relation which would then
have to be observed in the application of Nominal Extraposition
might be related to the case precedence relations which would also
have to be observed.

The anaphoric precedence relation can be stated quite simply:
the more antecedent nominal of a differentially-anaphoric pair
must be extraposed prior to the more anaphoric nominal. This can
be effected if and only if the subrules of (142) are applicable in a
sequential order such that the subrule applicable to a more antecedent nominal applies before the subrule applicable to a more
anaphoric nominal in any structure to which both subrules could
possibly be applied. Since the more antecedent member of a differentially-anaphoric pair is formally characterized as the member
with the longer species, the required restriction can be effected in an
entirely regular way if Nominal Extraposition is reformulated as

(143)   [[NOMINAL, W, (Z)], [VERB], X]
        ‾‾‾‾‾‾‾‾‾‾‾‾‾‾‾‾   ‾‾‾‾‾‾‾‾‾‾
                1   2   → [1, [2]],

where the parentheses around Z expositorily indicate, according to
a general convention for the analysis of conflated statements,[12]
a sequential ordering of the analyses:

[12]   See Chomsky (1967), Chomsky and Halle (1968). The X apparently has no

(144)   (i)   [[NOMINAL, W, Z], [VERB], X]
        (ii) [[NOMINAL, W], [VERB], X]

Since any structure that includes a differentially-anaphoric pair will have precisely these two analyses, and since analysis (i) will apply to the more antecedent member and analysis (ii) to the more anaphoric member, the correct anaphoric precedence hierarchy will be effected by the Nominal Extraposition conflation (143). The existence of this hierarchy with respect to this rule may thus appropriately be said to be explained as a necessary consequence of the general principles governing the formation and analysis of empirically significant conflations in conjunction with the independent fact that the representations of antecedents are always longer than those of their anaphoric reductions.

Let us turn now to the clearest instance of a non-anaphoric precedence relation with respect to Nominal Extraposition, namely, the precedence of Agents over Instrumentals. We may recall that both Agents and Instrumentals can occur as the most-extraposed, or most superordinate, nominal of a sentence, as in

(145)   (a)   John opened the door
        (b)   A golden key opened the door,

but that whenever an Agent and an Instrumental are associated in the same superficial clause, the Agent always takes precedence over the Instrumental with respect to the first application of Nominal Extraposition:

(146)   (a)   John opened the door with a golden key
        (b)   *A golden key opened the door with/by John

The problem then is to find some explanation for this particular

---

essential function in rule (143) and could be suppressed in accordance with a general convention to the effect that any reference to any constant A refers to any structure in which A is a non-subordinate (immediate) constituent. This convention has been widely employed in the formulation of rules specified in terms of multiple-valued and variable-valued features, and it has generally been assumed also with respect to the system of single-valued invariant feature notation that is employed here.

hierarchical relation, hopefully one which will also be compatible with the explanation of all other precedence relations which must be observed with respect to Nominal Extraposition.

The most obvious facts about Agents and Instrumentals are facts about their meanings and the relations that hold between their meanings. Thus both AGENT and INSTRUMENT are semantically complex, and, as suggested earlier by references to Agents as Animate Instruments and to Instruments as Inanimate Agents, they can reasonably be assumed to share at least one generic property in common. The characteristic obscurity of the boundary between so-called case properties and other generic properties is especially evident here too, however, and the distinction between Agents and Instruments can perhaps be assumed to consist solely of their distinction with respect to the property of Animateness. In any event let us assume, for present purposes, that Agents and Instruments are uniquely identified by the generic representations [INSTRUMENTAL, ANIMATE, x] and [INSTRUMENTAL, z], respectively, where z does not include ANIMATE.

Given these representations, it would then be possible to account for the extrapositional precedence of Agents over Instruments by means of a separate conflation of the form

(147)
$$[[\text{NOMINAL, INSTRUMENTAL, (ANIMATE)}], [\text{VERB}], X]$$
$$\underline{\hspace{4cm}1\hspace{4cm}}\quad\underline{\hspace{1cm}2\hspace{1cm}}$$
$$\rightarrow [1, [2]]$$

As in the parallel rule (143), the parentheses around the last constituent of the first term is to be understood as signifying an ordered sequence of analyses, the first here including the element ANIMATE, the second excluding it. Both the precedence of antecedents to their anaphoric reductions and that of animate instrumentals (Agents) to inanimate instrumentals can thus be accounted for in terms of fundamentally the same principle, the principle that more specific constituents take extrapositional precedence over less specific constituents of the same type. If all cases were like Agents and Instruments in having a fixed precedence rela-

tion and plausible semantic representations whereby the properties of a more precedent case properly include the properties of those which it is precedent to, then one might simply represent the set of cases of any language in a form such as [INSTRUMENTAL], [INSTRUMENTAL, ANIMATE], [INSTRUMENTAL, ANIMATE, RECIPIENT], [INSTRUMENTAL, ANIMATE, RECIPIENT, PATIENT], etc., and make use of a single multiple analysis conflation such as (148) to account for all precedence relations with respect to the process of nominal extraposition:

(148)   [[NOMINAL, INSTR, (ANIMATE, (REC, (PAT, (... (Z) ...))))]].[13]

However, the facts of the matter are obviously much more complex than this, first because the semantic relations between many pairs of cases are still exceedingly unclear, as are the various interactions between so-called case properties and properties of a

---

[13] It is assumed that all Predicatives (including Verbs) include among their inherent properties the generic properties of their possible arguments. This will allow for a very general and natural characterization of correct and incorrect axiomatic associations of substantives and predicatives on the basis of generic intersections of elements and the existence or non-existence of contradictions with respect to synthetic disjunctions of generic elements. (See Sanders 1967: Chapter 5.) Thus the relative grouping of nominals and predicatives is both grammatically significant and grammatically unpredictable, while the relative grouping of nominals with respect to other nominals is irrelevant both semantically and with respect to the proper characterization of correct and incorrect collocations. It appears, in other words, that the relative grouping of nominals is just as predictable as their relative ordering, and that the only axiomatic relations which need to be specified are the GROUPING RELATIONS BETWEEN LOGICAL ARGUMENTS AND THEIR LOGICAL PREDICATES.

The general principle of precedence-restricted extraposition suggested by rules such as (147) and (148) appears to be capable of extension in such a way as to block in the event of multiple instances of the same case, perhaps according to the Compatibility of Products constraint; it could probably also be extended in such a way as to allow certain multiple instances to be extraposed in random priority, to allow for the sort of treatment of symmetrical predications that has been proposed by Lakoff and Peters (1966). (But see, e.g. Tai [1969] for a more general and more strongly motivated treatment of symmetrical predications.) There are many other specific problems of collocation and case-precedence which have hardly been investigated at all yet, and this entire area promises to provide a very interesting and rewarding arena for future research.

more ordinary generic or temporal and locative character, but even more importantly perhaps because there are certain pairs of cases (e.g. Agent and Patient, Instrument and Patient) which have no apparent precedence relations at all when the cases are associated with anaphorically-unrelated nominals, but which do have such relations when the nominals are differentially anaphoric. We are back again, in other words, to the central problem of coreferential structuring, the problem of explaining how coreferentiality DETERMINES precedence relations with respect to the relative grouping of nominal constituents.

We have seen previously that Anaphora Formation can apply in a very general way to effect the proper reduction of a subordinate nominal in terms of a coreferential superordinate or coordinate nominal in any appropriately grouped structure. It is thus unnecessary to maintain the tentative assumption above that Anaphora Formation can apply before Nominal Extraposition. But if we return to the hypothesis that grouping precedes anaphoric reduction, we must assure that, in those structures to which Anaphora Formation can subsequently apply, Agents, for example, must be extraposed prior to Patients, while in other structures this particular precedence relation need not be observed at all. There appears to be at least one quite natural way of assuring this, a way which again employs the basic principle of specific precedence illustrated in the tentative anaphoric and case precedence extraposition rules (143) and (147).

In discussing the application of rule (143) above, it was assumed that the sequence of analyses which it conflates,

(148) (i) [[NOMINAL, W, Z], [VERB], X]
       (ii) [[NOMINAL, W], [VERB], X],

would identify the respective antecedent and anaphoric reduction of any differentially-anaphoric pair, and that the sequential application of the subrules of the conflation would thus correctly effect the prior extraposition of the antecedent member of any such pair. In discussing the Agent-Instrument precedence expressed by the second extraposition rule (147), it was noted that if the properties

of less precedent cases were properly included in those of more precedent cases, a similar precedence-determining conflation could be formulated, expressing another instance of the principle of more specific constituents taking precedence over less specific constituents.

Now prior to the application of Anaphora Formation all coreferential nominals are equally-anaphoric and precisely identical to each other EXCEPT FOR possible differences in their associated CASE properties. Thus any pair of coreferential nominals will be analyzable as

(149) [NOMINAL, W, x] [NOMINAL, W, y],

where x and y are case properties. If these sets of case properties happen to be related to each other in such a way that the constituents of x (say, A, B) are properly included in those of y (say, A, B, C), these nominals would then also be analyzable as

(150) [NOMINAL, $\underbrace{W, A, B}_{W'}$] [NOMINAL, $\underbrace{W, A, B,}_{W'}$ $\underset{Z}{\underline{C}}$]

and would hence be conflatable as (151a) representing the ordered sequence of analyses (151b) and (151c):

(151) (a) [NOMINAL, W' (Z)]
       (b) [NOMINAL, W', Z]
       (c) [NOMINAL, W']

Thus if Nominal Extraposition precedes Anaphora Formation a rule such as (143) would suffice to assure that for any pair of coreferential nominals the one with the more specific (i.e. properly including) case properties will always be extraposed prior to the one with the less specific (properly included) case properties.

It is evident then that if the case properties of Patients (say, [PARTICIPANT]) are properly included in those of Agents (say, [PARTICIPANT, MOTIVE, ANIMATE]), all Agents would be extraposed prior to coreferential Patients by rule (143), but either prior or subsequent to Patients which are not coreferential and thus not analyzable as [NOMINAL, W] with respect to the Agent's

analysis as [NOMINAL, W, Z]. The particular case analyses suggested here do not appear to be inherently implausible, but the ultimate correctness of these or any other analyses will depend, of course, on their semantic and syntactic appropriateness with respect to the entire network of precedence relations which underlie the observed alternations and non-alternations in the grouping and ordering of differentially-cased and differentially-anaphoric constituents in English and other languages.

We will thus rest our present case for the explanatory sufficiency of invariant derivational ordering at this point, and will conclude with an illustrative derivation of the sentence

(153)   Lucifer scratched himself with a pitchfork

in terms of the various general principles that have been proposed here.

(153)   Given: [[1], [2], [3], [4]]
        where: (1) = [NOMINAL, LUCIFER, PARTICIPANT,
                      MOTIVE, ANIMATE]
               (2) = [VERB, SCRATCHED]
               (3) = [NOMINAL, LUCIFER, PARTICIPANT,
                      ANIMATE]
               (4) = [NOMINAL, PITCHFORK, PARTICI-
                      PANT, MOTIVE]
        (a)   [[1], [2], [3], [4]]
              NOMINAL EXTRAPOSITION (143), 1st application
        (b)   [[1], [[2], [3], [4]]]
              NOMINAL EXTRAPOSITION (143), 2nd application[14]

---

[14]   We have not shown why an Instrumental should take precedence over a noncoreferential Patient, nor exactly how the case-precedence rule (147) can be fully subsumed by (143). It will be noted though that just as Agents (ANIMATE, PARTICIPANT, MOTIVE) properly include Instrumentals (PARTICIPANT, MOTIVE), the latter properly include Patients (PARTICIPANT). A generalized formulation of (147) would thus effectively assure the precedence of Instrumentals over Patients here and would thereby prevent the derivation of *Lucifer scratched with a pitchfork himself. A problem remains though with agentless sentences, in which the precedence relation between Patients and Instrumentals is apparently inoperative: A pitchfork scratched Lucifer, Lucifer was scratched with a pitchfork.

(c)   [[1], [[4], [[2], [3]]]]
NOMINAL EXTRAPOSITION (143), 3rd application

(d)   [[1], [[4], [[3], [[2]]]]]
ANAPHORA FORMATION (123), subordinate (3) reduced by (1)

(e)   [[1], [[4], [[3genus], [[2]]]]]
NOMINAL ORDERING (93), 1st application

(f)   [[1], [[4], [[[2]] & [3genus]]]]
NOMINAL ORDERING (93), 2nd application

(g)   [[1], [[[[2]] & [3genus]] & [4]]]
NOMINAL ORDERING (93), 3rd application

(h)   [[1] & [[[[2]] & [3genus]] & [4]]]
OTHER EXTRAPOSITIONS AND ORDERINGS (Clitics, Affixes, etc.)

(i)   [[1] & [[[[2 & PAST]] & [3genus]] & [WITH & ONE & 4]]]
LEXICAL RULES

(j)   [[*Lucifer*] & [[[[*scratch* & *ed*]] & [*himself*]] & [*with* & *one* & *pitchfork*]]]
PHONOLOGICAL RULES

(k)   [*Lucifer scratched himself with a pitchfork.*]

5

CONCLUSION

The Invariant Order Constraint asserts that the representations of a linguistic object cannot differ from each other in the order of their constituents. This constraint thus serves to limit the set of possible words, phrases, and sentences of natural languages by limiting the set of representational equivalence classes that constitute their formal linguistic definitions. It also serves to limit the set of possible grammars by excluding from this set all rule-sets that justify derivational reorderings of any sort or by any inferential means. As an empirical hypothesis about natural language, therefore, the Invariant Order Constraint has testable implications both with respect to the nature of the words, and sentences of natural languages, and with respect to the systems of human knowledge that underlie the systematic use of such objects for purposes of human communication.

Three critical tests of the Invariant Order principle have been conducted in the preceding chapters. The results of these tests indicate that the restrictions which are imposed by this principle are consistent with the known facts about natural languages and their range of possible variation. These results also strongly suggest that the assumption of invariant rather than variable ordering will have consistently greater value as a basis and stimulus for productive research in linguistics and for the discovery of significant explanatory generalizations in this domain.

The cases that have been dealt with here were chosen because of the apparent strength of the implicit arguments for reordering that were embodied in the original published analyses of the data

in question. The only comparably strong arguments for variable ordering that I know of are those implicit in the recent discussions of major constituent ordering in Amharic by Bach (1970) and in English by McCawley (1970). These arguments have also been successfully refuted now by Eckman (1972), Hochster (1973), Hudson (1972), and others. The refutation of all of these implicit arguments for reordering provides sufficient basis for considering the Invariant Order Constraint to be true now until proven otherwise.

Even without such evidence, in fact, the burden of proof would still rest necessarily with the proponents of variable ordering. This is the case, first, because of the apparent total lack of EXPLICIT arguments for derivational reordering in the linguistic literature. Thus in spite of the exceptionally widespread acceptance of the power of reordering by contemporary linguists, no real attempt has been made thus far to show that this power has any logical or empirical basis at all, or that it serves any necessary explanatory or heuristic function in theories of natural language. In fact, when constituent order has been explicitly discussed in the literature at all, the question of variable vs. invariant ordering has invariably been begged. Thus in discussions of this sort, as in Bach (1970), McCawley (1970), and Ross (1970), the powers of underlying ordering and derivational reordering are simply taken as given without question, and the only arguments that are presented are arguments for one underlying constituent ordering rather than another, or one set of reordering rules rather than another.[1] Since no reason is given for positing ANY underlying order of constituents in these cases or ANY derivational reorderings at all, these arguments can only be viewed as purely formalistic exercises that are deprived of any possible empirical basis or significance by their failure to exclude all of the alternatives to the positions advocated. Moreover, when the arguments are expanded to take account of

---

[1] Even on their own highly restricted terms, the arguments are often found to be either invalid or empirically non-significant. See, e.g. Hudson (1972) on Bach (1970); Hochster (1973) on McCawley (1970); and Koutsoudas (1971), Pulte (1971), and Sanders and Tai (1972) on Ross (1970).

the invariant order alternatives, as has been done here and in Hochster (1973), Hudson (1972), and a number of other recent studies, the data in question are found to provide no support at all for the orderings and reorderings originally proposed. They are found instead to provide support for the very theory of ordering that was not taken into consideration in the original arguments — the theory of invariant derivational ordering.

Actually, as far as I have been able to determine, there has been only one explicit attempt to justify ANY of the assumptions of the standard system of ordering and reordering incorporated in all standard theories of generative grammar. This is found in the very brief and inconclusive remarks on constituent ordering in Chomsky (1965: 123-127), where the power of reordering is again accepted without question or empirical support, and where the arguments that are given deal only with the relatively marginal question of whether ordering rules should or should not be conflated with the rules that specify the constituents of grammatical constructions. The two arguments that Chomsky gives on behalf of the conflation alternative are in fact both invalid — the first because it depends on a factual claim (that all alternate-order paraphrases have determinate derivational precedence relations) which is falsified by data from every known language (e.g. by pairs in English such as *John and Bill ran* and *Bill and John ran*); the second because it depends on a fact (that no natural language has both free ordering and free grouping of all superficial constituents) which is simply incapable of differentiating Chomsky's hypothesis of underlying ordering from the more natural hypothesis of superficial ordering, both of these hypotheses being equally consistent with both free- and non-free ordering, and neither having any implications at all with respect to free grouping. In any event, Chomsky has presented no arguments or evidence to show that postulations of derivational reorderings are necessary for the explanation of any facts about natural languages. Nor, as far as I can determine, has anyone else.

The lack of explicit arguments for derivational reordering, coupled with the successful refutation of the strongest known

implicit ones, clearly requires that the Invariant Order Constraint be assumed to be true now until proven otherwise. This assignment of the burden of proof is also dictated by the fact that this constraint determines a smaller and more homogeneous class of possible grammars and grammatical objects than can be determined by its contrary or contradictory. It thus provides for a narrower and more precise characterization of the set of possible natural languages and the set of possible systems of knowledge that could underlie their communicative uses in human societies. Pending evidence to the contrary, therefore, the Invariant Order Constraint must be assumed to be a true principle of natural language grammar which constitutes an essential part of the axiomatic basis of all possibly true grammatical theories or metatheories.

BIBLIOGRAPHY

Bach, E.
1968 "Two Proposals Concerning the Simplicity Metric in Phonology", *Glossa* 2, 128-149.
1969 "Anti-pronominalization" (Duplicated).
1970 "Is Amharic an SOV Language?", *Journal of Ethiopian Studies* 8, 9-20.

Chomsky, N.
1964a "The Logical Basis of Linguistic Theory", in H. G. Lunt (ed.), *Proceedings of the Ninth International Congress of Linguists* (The Hague: Mouton).
1964b "Current Issues in Linguistic Theory", in J. A. Fodor and J. J. Katz (eds.), *The Structure of Language*, 50-118 (Englewood Cliffs, N.J.: Prentice-Hall).
1965 *Aspects of the Theory of Syntax* (Cambridge: M.I.T. Press).
1967 "Some General Properties of Phonological Rules", *Language* 43, 102-138.
1970 "Remarks on Nominalization", in R. Jacobs and P. Rosenbaum (eds.), *Readings in English Transformational Grammar* (Boston: Ginn). Reprinted in N. Chomsky, *Semantics in Generative Grammar* (The Hague: Mouton, 1972).

Chomsky, N. and M. Halle
1968 *The Sound Pattern of English* (New York: Harper & Row).

Eckman, F.
1972 "Some Constraints on Pronominalization" (Indiana University doctoral dissertation).

Fillmore, C. J.
1966 "Towards a Modern Theory of Case", *Project on Linguistic Analysis* 13, 1-24 (The Ohio State University).

Gleitman, L. R.
1965 "Coordinating Conjunctions in English", *Language* 41, 260-293.

Hochster, A.
1973 "On Predicate Regrouping and Lexical Filtering" (University of Minnesota doctoral dissertation).

Hockett, C. F.
1954 "Two Models of Grammatical Description", *Word* 10, 210-231.

Hudson, G.
1972 "Why Amharic is Not a VSO Language", *Studies in African Linguistics* 3.1, 127-165.

Katz, J. J. and P. M. Postal
1964 *An Integrated Theory of Linguistic Descriptions* (Cambridge: M.I.T. Press).

Kiparsky, P.
1968 "Linguistic Universals and Linguistic Change", in E. Bach and R. Harms (eds.), *Universals in Linguistic Theory*, 170-202 (New York: Holt, Rinehart and Winston).

Koutsoudas, A.
1968 "On WH-Words in English", *Journal of Linguistics* 4, 267-273.
1971 "Gapping, Conjunction Reduction, and Coordination Deletion", *Foundations of Language* 7, 337-386.

Koutsoudas, A. (ed.)
1975 *The Ordering and Application of Grammatical Rules* (The Hague: Mouton).

Lakoff, G.
1968 "Pronouns and Reference" (Mimeographed, Indiana University Linguistics Club).

Lakoff, G. and P. S. Peters
1966 "Phrasal Conjunction and Symmetric Predicates", *Mathematical Linguistics and Automatic Translation*, Report No. NSF-17 (Cambridge: Harvard University Computation Laboratory).

Langacker, R. W.
1969a "On Pronominalization and the Chain of Command", in D. A. Reibel and S. A. Schane (eds.), *Modern Studies in English*, 160-186 (Englewood Cliffs, N.J.: Prentice-Hall).
1969b "Mirror Image Rules", *Language* 45, 575-598, 844-862.

McCawley, J. D.
1968 "The Role of Semantics in a Grammar". In E. Bach and R. T. Harms (eds.), *Universals in Linguistic Theory*, 124-169 (New York: Holt, Rinehart and Winston).
1970 "English as a VSO Language", *Language* 46, 286-299.

Norman, L. J.
1973 "Bidirectional Rules and Non-Extrinsic Ordering", Indiana University Conference on Rule Ordering (Mimeographed, Indiana University Linguistics Club). Reprinted in Koutsoudas (1975).

Perlmutter, D. M.
1968 "Deep and Surface Structure Constraints in Syntax" (M.I.T. doctoral dissertation).

Postal, P. M.
1968 "Coordination Reduction", Section III, Scientific Report 2, *Specification and Utilization of a Transformational Grammar* (Yorktown Heights, N.Y.: IBM).
1971 *Cross-Over Phenomena* (New York: Holt, Rinehart and Winston).

Pulte, W.
1971 "Gapping and Word Order in Quechua", in *Papers from the Seventh Regional Meeting of the Chicago Linguistic Society*, 193-197 (Chicago: Chicago Linguistic Society).

Ringen, C.
1973 "Vacuous Application, Iterative Application, Reapplication, and the Unordered Rule Hypothesis", Indiana University Conference on Rule Ordering (Mimeographed, Indiana University Linguistics Club). Reprinted in Koutsoudas (1975).

Ross, J. R.
1966 "A Proposed Rule of Tree-Pruning", *Mathematical Linguistics and Automatic Translation*, Report No. NSF-17 (Cambridge: Harvard University Computation Laboratory).
1967 "Constraints on Variables in Syntax", M.I.T. doctoral dissertation (Mimeographed, Indiana University Linguistics Club, 1968).
1969 "On the Cyclic Nature of English Pronominalization", in D. A. Reibel and S. A. Schane (eds.), *Modern Studies in English*, 187-200 (Englewood Cliffs, N.J.: Prentice-Hall).
1970 "Gapping and the Order of Constituents", in M. Bierwisch and K. E. Heidolph (eds.), *Progress in Linguistics*, 249-259 (The Hague: Mouton).

Sanders, G. A.
1967 "Some General Grammatical Processes in English", Indiana University doctoral dissertation. (Mimeographed, Indiana University Linguistics Club, 1968).
1970 "Precedence Relations in Language", paper presented at the Summer Meeting of the Linguistic Society of America, to appear in *Foundations of Language* 11 (1974), 361-400.
1972 *Equational Grammar* (The Hague: Mouton).
1973 "On the Exclusion of Extrinsic-Ordering Constraints", Indiana University Conference on Rule Ordering (Mimeographed, Indiana University Linguistics Club). Reprinted in Koutsoudas (1975).

Sanders, G. A. and J. H.-Y. Tai
1972 "Immediate Dominance and Identity Deletion", *Foundations of Language* 8, 161-198.

Schane, S. A.
1966 "A Schema for Sentence Coordination", Information System Language Studies No 10. (Bedford, Mass.: Mitre Corp.).

Tai, J. H.-Y.
1969 "Coordination Reduction". Indiana University doctoral dissertation (Mimeographed. Indiana University Linguistics Club, 1969).